The Alcohol Economy:
Fuel Ethanol and the
Brazilian Experience

The Alcohol Economy: Fuel Ethanol and the Brazilian Experience

Harry Rothman
Rod Greenshields
and
Francisco Rosillo Callé

Frances Pinter (Publishers), London

Copyright © Rothman, Greensheilds, Callé 1983

First published in Great Britain in 1983
by Frances Pinter (Publishers) Ltd,
5 Dryden Street, London WC2E 9NW

ISBN 0 86187 255 X

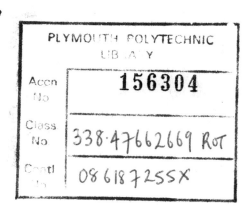
Typeset by Joshua Associates, Oxford, England
Printed in the United States of America

Dedication

To our families.
HR to Anne, Jake and Sean.
RNG to Erica.
FRC to Montse, Jordi, Sergio, Esther and Belén

CONTENTS

AUTHORS' NOTE

SI units have been used whenever possible, however in some instances primary sources are ambiguous in this respect and here units are quoted in the form in which they originally appeared. The use of the dollar symbol ($) denotes the US dollar unless otherwise stated, namely the Brazilian Cruzeiro, denoted as Cr$.

ACKNOWLEDGEMENTS

We are grateful to members of the Embassy of Brazil in London for allowing us to use the library facilities. We also thank individuals and organizations, too numerous to list, for sending us reprints and information. Our thanks to Dr. Dave Wield (Open University), Harold Mess and Zbigniew Towalski of the Technology Policy Unit for suggestions and for pointing out some of our mistakes; of course they are not responsible for any that remain. Special thanks to our typists, Mrs G. Crawford, Mrs O. Deeley, Mrs L. Doogan and Ms P. Taylor. We are also grateful to Professor Ernest Braun—Head of the Technology Policy Unit—for his support and friendly encouragement.

The Federal Republic of Brazil

INTRODUCTION

Pierre Mariotte, President of the French *Société du Petrole Vert*, expressed the dilemma of many Third World countries concerned about their future supplies of petroleum as follows:

Do nothing and wait for some miraculous help, incurring the risk of ever increasing oil prices and eventual rationing by the suppliers. Or exploit national and renewable resources as quickly as possible in order to be ready to face an uncertain and uncontrollable future for oil resources.

Brazil has chosen *to act* through the *Programa Nacional do Álcool* (PNA). This book is about the Brazilian national alcohol programme; its policies, technologies and social and economic aspects, its problems as well as successes. We have brought together diverse material from scattered sources in an endeavour to clarify this unique political and technical experiment, whose goal as expressed by its most ardent supporters is an 'ethanol economy', in which vegetable matter—biomass—is used to ferment ethanol as a renewable resource so as to reduce reliance upon non-renewable petroleum. This remarkable achievement, now well into its eighth year, is the creation of the Third World, and perhaps because of this has not been given the attention it deserves.

We hope that this work will make the Brazilians' efforts and experiences more widely known; not only to active researchers, innovators and students, who will improve on what has already been achieved, but especially to political and commercial decision makers and the wider public—for without their clear understanding and support nothing will change.

1 TOWARDS THE ETHANOL ECONOMY

1.1 The Vulnerability of the Petroleum Economy

Today's chemical industries—which provide plastics, pharmaceuticals, textile fibres, agricultural chemicals and innumerable other essential consumer and industrial products—are largely based upon petroleum as a primary raw material. Contemporary industrial society is in truth a 'petroleum economy'. This has not always been the case. Prior to the mid-nineteenth century agriculture and other biologically-based sources provided our organic materials. Then Perkin's synthesis of the first dye-stuff from coal in 1856 signalled our entry into a 'coal economy'. It was not until the 1920s that the first petrochemical was developed—isopropyl alcohol. Even in 1940, 95% of the 3 million tons of organic chemicals then produced came from coal, and just 5% from petroleum. However, the coal economy soon reached its zenith and although by 1978 overall organic chemical production was up a hundredfold to 340 million tons only 3% originated from coal, whereas 97% was petroleum based.

Our reliance upon the petroleum economy is emphasized further by the facts that our transport systems by land, sea and air are almost wholly dependent on petroleum energy products, and a very high percentage of the world's electricity is generated by oil-fuelled power stations.

It is now clear that the predominance of the petroleum economy cannot last for more than a few more decades. Indeed perhaps its demise is already on the horizon. For the most significant effect of the decision by OPEC (Oil Petroleum Exporting Countries) to increase oil prices in the summer of 1973 has been to expose the vulnerability of an industrial world based in the main on a single commodity owned and controlled by a relatively few nations. Today crude oil costs 700% more than it did before the OPEC decision. Despite short-term fluctuations, further price increases are virtually assured. The long-term future could be bleak. The International Energy Agency (an OECD body) has predicted that by the year 2000 the OECD could have a deficit of $1-4 \times 10^9$ tons of petroleum units.

It is now clear that the 'oil crisis' is not only an energy crisis but also a crisis of chemical resources. It is, thus, of considerable importance that substitution of petroleum as an energy source should be studied intensively on a world-wide basis. Innovation to command access to feed stocks and other resources of organic chemicals are thus an absolute necessity, and the novel biomass alternatives are being studied and evaluated not only as energy sources but also as alternative sources for chemical feedstocks.

Coal and agricultural products are most likely to follow petroleum as primary sources of chemical feedstock and fuels —the rate of substitution will depend largely upon the price of oil, but also on the ease with which they are converted into basic chemicals that fit into present petrochemical processing systems. For a major advantage of petroleum as chemical feedstock has been that a few simple chemical compounds, which can be converted into a wide variety of chemical products, can be produced in large, centralized, highly economical petrochemical refineries.

1.2 The Biotechnological Alternative

Biotechnology is the multidisciplinary study of the commercial exploitation of biological materials, living organisms and their activities; in effect '. . . a catch word for the new forms of chemical engineering concerned with the industrial utilization of cellular, microbial and enzyme processes' (Rothman *et al.*, 1981; Greenshields and Rothman, 1982). A study group has recently completed a report for the Commission of the European Communities (FAST, 1982) which examines a long-term (25–30 years) scenario for a 'bio-society' in which significant sections of productive activities are based upon the techniques and products of biotechnology. The choice of the 'bio-society' for their long-term scenario partly reflects the exciting prospects of applying the New Biology, but the dominant reason for choosing it was that the bio-society was regarded as '. . . the most promising basis for a *sustainable*, secure and prosperous future' (FAST, 1979, p. 3). Over the last five years country after country has published official reports extolling the potential of biotechnology (see for example ACARD, 1980). Ethanol, produced by fermenting biomass (organic/plant matter), is widely regarded as especially promising.

1.3 Brazil and the Ethanol Economy

The most ambitious biotechnology programme actually being applied on a national scale is to be found in Brazil—a Third World nation. The Brazilians have concentrated their efforts chiefly in a single field of biotechnology—the fermentation of ethanol from biomass for use as an energy source and as a chemical feedstock. Through their national alcohol programme, *Programa Nacional do Álcool* (PNA) Brazil has entered the 'ethanol economy' with a determination unmatched elsewhere.

In the following chapters we bring together much scattered information about the PNA, describing how Brazil came to develop such an ambitious programme; the technical and economic aspects; and its implications for other countries considering the potential of the ethanol economy.

It is first necessary to answer the question why ethanol? After all for the non-specialist it is chiefly enjoyed as a beverage! For the industrialist, however, ethanol is one of the most commercially versatile organic compounds known. It can be burned as an energy source, it can be used as a chemical feedstock from which a wide range of important organic compounds can be derived, it has many other unique properties—for example as a solvent, germicide, antifreeze (see Appendix 2). Such is its versatility that one can foresee, in certain circumstances, an 'ethanol economy' in which ethanol could play a role analogous to that presently played by petroleum.

1.4 Ethanol Properties and Production (Kirk and Othmer, 1980)

Ethanol is the International Union of Pure and Applied Chemistry (IUPAC) name for this chemical although ethyl alcohol is still a widely used term. In scientific terms alcohol is used to describe a class of organic compounds which has an hydroxyl as a functional group but particularly the alkanes where a hydrogen is substituted with an hydroxyl group CnH_2n+_2O or CnH_2n+_1OH. Because the second member of the alkane series, ethanol, has such a wide use in commerce and consumed as a beverage it has been given a wide variety of other names as well as just the prime name ethyl alcohol or alcohol. For example, spirits of wine, eau de vie, aqua vitae, cologne spirits, white spirit, grain spirit, petroleum spirit etc.

The word alcohol is of Arabic derivation, 'al-Koh'l (al 'the' and Koh'l 'powder'). Indeed Koh'l was a powder, probably powdered antimony, which was used to paint and decorate eyebrows in the East and later came to describe any fine powder. However, one authority points out that none of the Arab scientists actually mentions distilling alcohol until the thirteenth century, and then the word used is not 'alcohol' but 'al-raqa' from which the word 'arak' is taken, meaning 'sweat'. The modern word and meaning came many centuries later. Paracelsus (a pseudonym used by Theophrastus Bombastus von Hohenheim—and why not!) and Libavius both used the term to denote a very fine powder though Libavius also used it to describe an alcohol derived from an antimony salt. Paracelsus used the term subsequently also to denote a volatile liquid but *alcool* and *alcool vini* occur often in his later writing and he once adds *'id est vino ardente'* ('it is strong wine').

Alcohol has been a favoured component of beverages since time immemorial. Babylonian relics indicate at least 6000 years but probably it is as old as when man settled to an agricultural existence in Europe after the third ice age some 10000 years ago. It was well known to the Egyptians and also to the Romans and Arabs before the time of Christ. By AD 800 monks were producing substantial amounts of fermented liquors in Europe both as a means to refresh themselves and for income. Nevertheless it was not until the nineteenth and twentieth centuries that it became important in its own right on a substantial scale.

Ethanol can be derived by fermentation processes from any material in which the carbohydrate is present in the form of sugar, although currently most industrial processes use a petroleum by-product—ethylene—to produce ethanol. Fermentation is thus one of man's oldest chemical processes, producing an enormous variety of commodities from food to chemical products. Many systems have been developed to release the potential of biomass energy, but they all utilize one of two basic principles—thermochemical or biological conversion. Thermochemical techniques use heat and pressure to provoke a chemical reaction in the biomass to produce fuels such as synthesis gas, ammonia, hydrogen and carbon monoxide. Bioconversion uses enzymes, fungi or other micro-organisms to release the stored energy. Depending upon the specific process employed, this type of system will yield either ethanol or methane gas.

The chemical industry presently relies upon four main chemical and microbial processes for converting biomass into basic chemicals.

(a) *Fermentation* is the microbial conversion of sugar and starch contained in plant material. It leads directly (or in the case of starch, after enzymatic hydrolysis), to ethanol, carbon dioxide and other by-products.
(b) *Pyrolysis* of wood (thermal cracking in the absence of air) leads to methanol, acetic acid and charcoal.
(c) *Partial oxidation* of wood or cellulosic waste gives a mixture of hydrogen and carbon monoxide similar to synthesis gas.
(d) *Hydrolysis* of wood (chemical or enzymatic) forms sugar which can be further fermented to give ethanol.

However, the fermentation step is the prime process for alcohol production and the majority of the research effort to date has gone into this area. Alcoholic fermentation has traditionally been a batch process and still remains so, with only a few exceptions. Continuous steady-stage fermentation would present many advantages since the lag phase and the growth of the yeast, which accounts for a large part of the cycle time in the batch fermentation, would be eliminated. When the raw material has been converted to fermentation sugars, then these are fermented typically with yeast to give a broth containing 6–12% ethanol with small amounts of aldehydes, ketones, amylalcohols and methanol (fusel oils). The final step, distillation to give water-free alcohol, is an energy consuming process—between 50% and 60% of all energy used in a typical fermentation ethanol manufacturing process. However new process technology is being developed which will reduce this energy cost considerably.

To recover ethanol from the fermentation broth is at least a three-step process:

1 distillation of the dilute alcohol to its azeotrope (95–57% ethanol by weight);
2 distillation utilizing a third component (either an organic solvent or a strong dehydrating agent) to break up the azeotrope and remove the remaining water;
3 distillation to separate water from the third component to give absolute alcohol and allow the third component to be recycled (Ladisch and Dick, 1979).

Industrial ethanol is produced, (a) synthetically from ethylene, (b) as a by-product of certain industrial operations, and (c) by the fermentation of sugar, starch and cellulose materials. Before 1930 ethanol was produced by industrial processes employing natural fermentation. There are two main processes for the synthesis of ethanol from ethylene. The first to be developed in 1930 by Union Carbide was the indirect hydration or esterification hydrolysis process. The other synthesis process which eliminates the use of sulphuric acid, is referred to as the direct hydration process.

Until the early 1940s the production of industrial ethanol by fermenting crops was widespread in Europe, chiefly from corn potatoes and sugar beets. After 1945 fermentation in the industrial chemical market was replaced by petroleum based sources as petroleum gradually became relatively cheaper in the post-war years. Governments began to withdraw subsidies to national alcohol production programmes and by 1950 nearly all facilities were terminated, except in a few countries like Argentina, Brazil, India and the Philippines where some production continued on a small scale.

The direct hydration process has already completely supplanted the old sulphuric acid process since the early 1970s. The current synthetic production of industrial alcohol far exceeds its production by fermentation. Industrial ethanol production is often under government monopoly.

1.5 Why Brazil?

In 1973 *The Times* said of Brazil: 'Like a sleeping giant Brazil is awakening to a period of industrial expansion and development almost unparalleled among countries of the Third World.' Of course, this is not a truly correct image of Brazilian economic history, but it does serve to draw attention to the so-called economic miracle engineered since the military coup which destroyed the civilian government in 1964.

Brazil's drive towards industrialization over the last 20 years has been enormous and this, together with the country's great natural resources and sheer territorial size, make it likely that Brazil will be a major power in the not too distant future. Figure 1.1 (Appendix 1) gives the basic natural statistics that illustrate this potential. It has a population of 122 million, a gross national product of 285.4×10^9, and a sizeable industrial-goods production, for example, in 1979 Brazil produced about 14 million tons of steel; nearly 300 aircraft; 1.1 million motor vehicles; and 63000 tractors. Such production already rivals that of some developed countries; indeed, Brazil is already one of the largest ship builders in the world.

Brazil is beginning to have influence far beyond South America itself. Recently Brazil sold 400 armoured vehicles to Iraq worth $200 million. If these vehicles do well it will be able to consolidate itself as an arms exporter—presently Brazil is the seventh-largest arms exporter in the world. But its activities go beyond that: Brazil has been working hard to win markets in the Third World. The Brazilian salesmen have been quick to point out that they represent a country whose technology is better adapted to the needs of the Third World. These efforts have not been wholly in vain, since nowadays Brazil is exporting vehicles to Nigeria, arms to Togo, and many others, its technicians have sought and found oil in Iraq, are working on a 1×10^9 rail contract to link Baghdad to the Syrian border and are selling alcohol distillery technology to the United States. By the end of 1979, the Brazilians were involved in twenty major export construction projects, in some fifteen countries, worth over 4×10^9.

Nevertheless Brazil, despite such industrial progress, is a country of great contrasts—socioeconomic and regional differences are huge. Demographic data projections are found in Appendix 1, which show the estimated population from 1950-2000 by age group; urban and rural population; and distribution by regions. These differences will be the source of major political and economic difficulties in the years to come.

Brazil is still under military rule although recently, under the Presidency of General Figueiredo, there are signs of a relaxation and an opening up of democratic channels. There are also signs that the pattern of development that successive governments have followed for more than a decade are becoming increasingly less viable. Indeed, much of the economic success occurred in the period prior to the world recession of 1974-75, and Brazil emerged from the recession with enormous foreign debts.

Brazil's current foreign debt is the largest in the Third World—some 64.5×10^9 and rising (some estimates put it a bit lower). The cost of servicing the debts in 1982 is estimated to be 19×10^9 (10×10^9 in interest payments and 9×10^9 in amortizations).

The trade deficit during the first half of 1980 was 2.2×10^9 and at the end of December 1980 the balance was 12×10^9 in the red. Thus the balance of payments has become a pressing problem. Oil consumption, despite government efforts to reduce imports, continues to grow. In 1981 it was estimated that 0.6-0.7 million barrels per day would be imported and in 1980 oil imports accounted for 46% of the value of all imports.

Foreign oil dependence has been an increasingly serious problem for Brazil, particularly since the oil crisis of 1973. The extent of this dependence came especially clear when the Iran/Iraq war broke out, and the government was forced to look in desperation for alternative oil suppliers.

Brazil must import 45% of its energy needs—from a mere $223 million in 1969, $7 × 10⁹ in 1979 (44% of its total imports and 47% of its export value) to circa $11 × 10⁹ in 1980. Figure 1.1 shows this increase of imports of oil related to the total income of the Brazilian exports for the period 1970 to 1979.

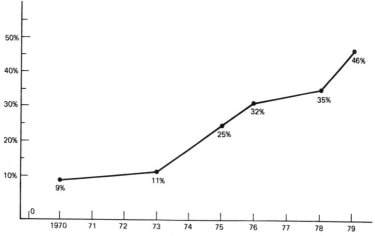

Fig. 1.1   Percentage of the expenses with importation of crude oil related to total income of the Brazilian exports.

The goal for 1985 is to limit oil consumption to the equivalent of 1.5 million barrels per day (mbd) of oil, of which only 0.5 mbd would be imported. An assumption seen by many as over optimistic—such estimates put domestic oil production at 370000 barrels per day and alcohol at 90000 barrels per day. Approximately 1.0 million barrels per day (equivalent) would be produced domestically of which 0.5 mbd would be domestic oil production; 170000 barrels per day of sugarcane alcohol; 170000 barrels per day of coal; 120000 barrels per day of wood alcohol, 25000 barrels per day of shale oil and another 15000 barrels per day derived from other sources.

Unlike the developed countries Brazil depends overwhelmingly on road transport since the country does not possess a railway system of any substance. Fuel and diesel oil demand rose by almost 10% in 1979. Thus the government has been forced to initiate a programme with the purpose of modifying this consumption pattern. The alternative Transport Programme for Fuel Economy has been launched requiring Cr\$133.0 $\times$ 10^9 in 1980/2 of which Cr\$91.2 $\times$ 10^9 will be channelled into urban transportation systems and Cr\$41.8 $\times$ 10^9 will be for cargo transport. This shows that it is not merely a question of trying to reduce oil imports *per se* but that other internal structural changes must be borne in mind as well. (For further details on Brazilian energy resources see Appendix 1.)

Inflation has begun to soar again and is now running at over 100%. Rising costs of oil derivatives and agricultural production, once heavily subsidized, are now being allowed to reach their 'natural level' and are being blamed for the latest rise in inflation.

Some commentators believe that such economic failures may lead to increasing social unrest and that this may strengthen the hand of those who oppose the current political relaxation policy. National elections are due in 1982; the manner in which they are conducted will be the test of whether Brazil has successfully made the transition to a democratic regime.

Nevertheless, although seriously stricken by the effects of the crises, Brazil now stands, potentially, as one of the few countries in a position to overcome the difficulties, and even draw some degree of advantage from them, due to their immense energy potential. The most significant factors in Brazil's favour are: sheer territorial size; an extremely long coast-line; favourable geological composition; a voluminous hydrographic basin; and enormous arable land area with an advantageous tropical geographic location, plus intense sunlight for maximum plant growth; and a large agricultural labour supply.

References

ACARD (1980), 'Biotechnology: A report of a joint working party', Advisory Council for Applied Research and Development, Advisory Board for Research Councils, The Royal Society, HMSO, London.

Bôto Dantas, R. (1980), 'Production of alcohol: the Brazilian experience', *International Sweetner Alcohol Conference: The Future of Sugar*, April, London.

British Chamber of Commerce in Brazil (1980), 'Foreign capital and the alcohol sector', *Information Circular*, No. 18, 30 September.

Büchel, K. H. (1980), 'Agricultural products—raw material and energy source of the future', *Chemistry International*, No. 5, 17-25.

Coulson-Thomas, C. (1980), 'Brazil business opportunities in the 1980s', *Metra Consulting Group and International Joint Ventures.*

European Brazilian Bank (1980), 'Brazil: Land of the present', London.

FAST (1979), 'Sub-Programme C–Bio-society', Commission of the European Communities, DG XII, FAST/ACPM/79/14-3E, Brussels.

FAST (1982), 'Strategic issues for Europe in the long-term development and potential application of biotechnology', Commission of the European Communities, DG XII, XII-0041-82, Brussels.

Financial Times (1980), 'Brazil (A Survey)', 14 November.

Greenshields, R. and Rothman, H. (1982), 'Biotechnology: applications in Third World countries', FAST Colloquium, 2-4 Feb., *Centre Science, Technologie et Société*, Paris.

Kirk, R. E. and Othmer, D. F. (1980), 'Ethanol', in *Encyclopaedia of Chemical Technology*, Vol. 8.

Ladisch, M. B. and Dick, K. (1979), 'Dehydration of ethanol, new approach gives positive energy balance', *Science*, **205** (4409), 898-900.

Latin American Weekly Report (1981). 'Cursing the cannibalistic bankers', 2 October.

Lewis, C. W. (1980), 'Alcohol and methane, two biological fuels for man', *The Biologist*, **27** (2), 68-72.

Lloyds International (1980), 'Brazil', *Bank of London and South America Review*, **14**, August.

Rothman, H. *et al.* (1981), *Biotechnology: A Review and Annotated Bibliography*, Frances Pinter (Publishers) Ltd, London.

Schwartz, R. (1980), 'Fuel from fields', *Showcase USA* **2** (4), 10-15.

Shires, M. J. and Gellender, M. (1980), 'Gasified coal, starting point for chemical manufacture', *Chemistry International*, No. 6, 5-11.

The Times (1973), 18 October, 1, London.

Trebat, J. J. (1980), 'Brazil: the miracle is over, but some good work may begin', *Euromoney*, April, **37**.

US Department of Commerce, Industry and Trade Administration (1979), *Overseas Business Reports* OBR **16**, June, Washington DC.

2 POWER ALCOHOL IN BRAZIL

2.1 Historical

Alcohol has been utilized in Brazil for many decades, first as a combustible and then as a chemical feedstock.

Prior to the creation of the National Alcohol Programme (PNA) in 1975, the alcohol industry has always been determined by outside factors, strictly speaking it was a by-product of the sugar industry. The sugar industry played a vital role in the Brazilian economy and government policy towards it is of fundamental importance to understanding and development of the alcohol industry.

Government intervention has been dictated by the need to rationalize sugar production, and alcohol was seen as one of the instruments by which this rationalization could be carried out. This strong state intervention has been particularly relevant since the early 1930s. After the World Crisis of 1929 the Brazilian sugar industry—the oldest in the country—was in a chaotic situation. As a remedy the *Commissão de Defesa da Produçao do Açúcar* was created, later to be replaced by the *Instituto do Açúcar e do Álcool* (IAA). By that time alcohol was seriously seen by some experts and in some government circles as a potential help to the solution of the sugar problem, and also as a petroleum substitute. The prevailing cheap oil prices prevented the alcohol industry from being anything other than a by-product of the sugar sector until the late 1970s when it acquired an independent status. Table 2.1 summarizes the major political developments and forecasts of the alcohol industry. (For 1980–85 see also Table 3.2.)

Table 2.1   Political evolution of the alcohol economy

Date	Observations
(2) 1973	Experiments at the Fuels and Minerals Testing Centre with Otto engines powered by neat alcohol.
(1) 20.2.1931	Decree No. 19717 makes a minimum of 5% blend of alcohol with imported gasoline compulsory.
(1) 4.8.1931	The Ministry of Agriculture created a commission to study ethanol for automotive fuel.
(1) 7.12.1931	Decree No. 20761 creates the Commission of Defence for Alcohol Production.
(4) 24.3.1932	Decree No. 31301 authorizes the Ministry of Agriculture to assign contracts to support sugar-mills for pure alcohol production.
(3) 4.6.1932	Decree No. 21531 authorizes the Ministry of Agriculture to maintain a distribution system of ethyl alcohol.
(4) 1.6.1933	Decree No. 22789 establishes the Institute of Sugar and Alcohol (IAA): Support for alcohol blending in combustion engines.
(2) 1938	Federal legislation approves extending the compulsory addition of anhydrous ethanol also to gasoline refined in Brazil.
(4) 22.9.1942	Decree-Law No. 4722 considered the alcohol-based industry to be of national interest and established the minimum price for alcohol, and its raw materials (for a minimum period of 4 years).
(2) 1942/1956	Average annual ethanol content in ethanol/gasoline blends reaches 40% in North Eastern Brazil.
(2) 1956/1960	Ethanol/gasoline blends fluctuate according to international sugar price.
(1) 1960/1965	High sugar prices in the international market and low petroleum prices reduced the role of ethanol fuels in Brazil. Law No. 4.452 modified tax legislation on fuels introducing an additional one on alcohol.
(1) 1966/1967	Low sugar prices in the international market. Decree No. 59.190 (08/09/66) authorized the upper limit of alcohol/gasoline blends from 5% to 10%.

Date	Observations
(1) 1973/1974	Steep increases in petroleum prices. Beginning of experiments by CTA (Aerospace Technical Centre) on higher percentage ethanol/gasoline blendings.
(2) 14.11.75	Decree No. 76593 creates the National Alcohol Programme (PNA) to promote ethanol production from different sources. Alcohol to displace more of Brazil's gasoline demand.
(2) 1977	Beginning of fleet tests of neat-ethanol car engines (Otto) based on CTA experiments. Annual alcohol production 1.4 million m^3—45% added to gasoline to deploy 5% of Brazil's gasoline demand.
(2) 1978	About fifty blending centres supplying ethanol/ gasoline blends in Brazil. Product: 2.4 million m^3— 60% added to gasoline displacing 11% of Brazil's gasoline demand.
(2) 1979	Beginning of the manufacture of neat ethanol cars by automotive industry and selling of neat alcohol fuel at public service stations. Production: 3.7 million m^3—60% added to gasoline replacing 14% of Brazil's demand.
(2) 1980	Purchase of neat alcohol (retrofilling is allowed to general public). Production about 4 million m^3.
(2) 1982	Annual ethanol production: 5.5 million m^3; neat ethanol car population, 1.2 million projected units (Otto engines) or 10% of total passenger cars.
(2) 1985	Annual ethanol production target: 10.7 million m^3. Ethanol to displace gasoline, plus 1.5 million m^3 the chemical industry.

Sources: (1) Maura Leitão (1979).
(2) Goldstein, L. et al. (1980).
(3) I simposio Sobre Produçao de Alcool No Noreste (Fortaleza 10th–12th August 1977).
(4) Oliveira (1979).

2.2 Criteria for Alcohol Production

It has become imperative to find ways to escape from over-dependence on petroleum as an energy source and chemical feedstock. Biomass processing has begun to be seen as a promising route to an alternative source of energy and chemical feedstock. There are many reasons why Brazil is actively involved in this new field and is committing itself to large-scale biomass production. These form the basic criteria of any country considering a biomass-energy scenario.

Brazil possesses abundant land, suitable climate, an agricultural vocation and a historical experience in alcohol production and a need, appreciated at high government levels, to reduce national dependence on oil. Few countries possess the natural resources to rival Brazil's biomass potential.

2.3 The Biomass Alternative

Biomass is simply organic matter and in practice it covers many things: from the raw materials of alcohol production to trees which can be milked for an oil-like sap; from garbage which can be converted to gas to combustible forest wastes.

The potential of biomass is enormous. Figure 2.1 illustrates the concept of an integrated cyclic fermentation system running from the agricultural sector to and through the light, medium and heavy industrial sectors over the whole structure of the nation—a concept considered by the EEC FAST Programme as the Bio-society (FAST, 1979). Living plants trap more than ten times the total energy consumed by man, but only a fraction of this energy could be tapped. Nevertheless this biomass source could make a sizeable contribution to energy requirements and since this biomass is renewable it makes a continuing contribution. In monetary terms the EEC FAST programme estimates that the Bio-society is 40% of an industrialized society and probably more in Third World countries such as Brazil.

The options offered by biomass are important partly because it is a widely distributed source of fuel and one for which many developing countries have the essential resources in abundance. World-wide potential of, for example, crop wastes and animal manure is just over 3×10^9 tons annually—

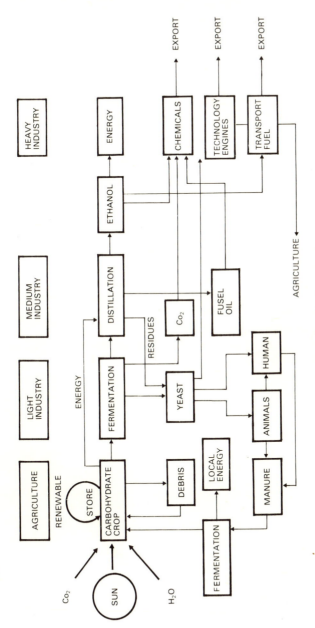

Fig. 2.1 Integrated cyclic fermentation system.

with an energy content of 25% of present world energy consumption—and in the case of non-OPEC developing nations, which contain 40% of the world's population, this non-commercial fuel often comprises up to 90% of their total energy needs.

In practice, however, matters are quite different and biomass potential should not be overestimated, because energy from biomass is difficult to recover, the total availability is far smaller; on the other hand to replace just 1 million barrels of oil each day is said to require some twenty large synthetic fuel plants at a cost of between $1-2 \times 10^9$ at 1979 prices.

The relative advantages and disadvantages of using biomass for energy vary throughout the world depending on the level of industrial and agricultural development, *per capita* consumption, availability of land, its quality and solar radiation. To be competitive at least for some time to come, energy from biomass would depend primarily on the integration of fuel production. To use it to produce fuel only would be uncompetitive and morally wrong, bearing in mind food shortages.

We can summarize the advantages and disadvantages of biomass as an energy source as follows (Hall, 1979; Goodman and Pimentel, 1979):

Advantages—the main advantages of biomass are:
1 Stores energy for use at will;
2 It is renewable;
3 Versatile conversion and products;
4 Dependent on technology already available with minimum capital input;
5 Can be developed with present manpower and material sources;
6 Reasonably priced, at least for some countries;
7 Ecologically inoffensive and safe;
8 Does not increase atmospheric CO_2.

Disadvantages—its major disadvantages include:
1 Land-use depletion;
2 Large land areas required;
3 Uncertain supply in initial stages;

4 Fertilizer, soil and water requirements are high;
5 The relatively small amount of high energy converted into biomass by plants;
6 Relatively low concentration of biomass per unit of land and water;
7 High moisture content (75-95%) of biomass that makes collection and transport expensive and energy conversion inefficient.

2.4 The Energy Crops

The many varied raw materials used in the manufacture of ethanol via fermentation are conveniently classified under three types of agricultural raw materials:

1 *Sugars*—(from sugarcane, sugar beet, molasses and fruit) may be converted to ethanol directly. Sucrose is one of the most abundant carbohydrates; it is mostly consumed either directly or in manufactured goods or in animal feeds, but only a small portion is actually utilized as a chemical feedstock to produce sucrose esters. None the less, as a chemical feedstock it has several useful advantages, since it can be obtained as a pure defined organic compound of relatively low molecular weight with a multiple chemical functionality giving the molecule a high potential for versatile application and capable of being produced cheaply.

2 *Starches*—(from grains, potatoes and root crops) must first be hydrolyzed to fermentable sugars by action of enzymes from malt or moulds. The production of glucose from starch is a major industry, but total production was in 1975 just 4.65 million tons. Chemically modified starches are becoming increasingly important as new applications are developed—in addition to the wide range of chemical products already being produced. Starch derivatives are essentially produced by the partial reaction of the hydroxyl groups of starch to give esters or ethers.

3 *Cellulose*—(from wood, agriculture wastes, waste sulphite, liquor from pulp mills which contain sugar derived from cellulose and the hemicellulose hydrolysis) must likewise be

converted to sugars, in this case by the action of mineral acids. Wood is the single most important source—its composition is about 40–50% cellulose, 20–30% lignin and 20–35% hemicelluloses, depending upon the species and conditions of growth. Cellulose presents problems, for example, as a chemical feedstock, since it is a polymer of the simple sugar glucose into which it can be converted on hydrolysis, but its resistance to breakdown either by acid or enzymes from fungi, without considerable expenditure of energy in milling, makes it uneconomic. Cellulose is not currently used as a feedstock, except for the production of regenerated cellulose fibres and films, or chemically modified cellulose derivatives.

A summary of the yields from the various energy crops is shown on Table 2.2, including the ethanol yield, and ethanol required to produce some of the chemical products. This table is intended as an overview and therefore the yield differential round the world must also be borne in mind.

Of all energy crops mentioned, sugarcane produced the highest alcohol yield per hectare with yields reaching between 3800–12000 l/ha/a. This range reflects the fact that normally old and conventional techniques are used. Sugarbeet, sorghum, cassava, potatoes also provide high yields.

Sweet sorghum has a great potential as an energy crop particularly in the temperate zone. It typically yields 3554 l/ha/a of alcohol which could easily be increased with a modest investment.

Among cereals there is little variation in the rate of conversion to alcohol. Wheat, corn and grain sorghum all yield about the same amount of alcohol per bushel of grain— 2.6 gal for wheat.

It should be stressed that the great variation in alcohol yield/ha/yr derives almost entirely from the widely varying cereal yield/ha in the different parts of the world.

2.5 Energy Crops in Brazil

Several raw materials are being considered to obtain alcohol on a large scale, particularly saccharineous materials such as sugarcane and sorghum and starchy plants such as cassava and babassu. Table 2.3 shows the main sources being considered for alcohol production from an agricultural and industrial standpoint. The figures indicated correspond to average values prevailing in Brazil (in 1979)—at national levels there exist higher fluctuations. A brief description of each of these main crops follows:

1 *Sugarcane (*Saccharum officianale*) (Fig. 2.4).*

By far the most important and immediate source for alcohol production today in Brazil (as well as in the past) is sugarcane. Alcohol production began in the 1930s after government intervention to protect the sugar sector. In the short term it is almost the exclusive source for ethanol.

In typical tropical climates, about 10% of the cane weight can be recovered as crystalline sucrose, but actual recoveries vary from as little as 6% to as high as 14%.

Sugarcane offers a series of advantages such as the existence of a sucro-industry, and a domestic agricultural and industrial technology. It is a semi-perennial crop, capable of producing a 'ratoon' (regrowth) crop from stubble left at harvest. Stands of cane exist which were planted up to 20 years ago, and increases in the price of tractor fuel may encourage more prolonged ratooning. However, with prolonged ratooning yields may decrease. In the case of Brazil there exists plenty of room for mechanization, by which it is possible, at not very high cost, to improve yields significantly. The energy balance is positive in most of the cases and by-product molasses can also be used for producing alcohol. Sugarcane has a higher than average photosynthetic efficiency.

With the agro-industrial productivity obtained in the last 10 years, the Brazilian molasses show a total content of reducing sugars ranging from 52 to 62% which can result, when conveniently processed, in 280–333 litres of alcohol/ton of cane. Its fermentation process is simple and takes

Table 2.2 Energy crop—ethanol yields

	Sugar cane	Sugar beets	Cassava (Manioc) (Tapioca)	Potatoes	Maize	Paddy rice	Wheat	Sweet sorghum (stem only)[3]	Grain sorghum (grain only)[2]	Starch[4]	Molasses[5]
Crop Yield t/ha/a[1]											
Commercial mean	80	50	10	13.99	2.95	2.57	1.66	35	7.5[2]		
Realistic range	50–120	30–80	6–30+	11–32	1.0–5.1	1.8–5.3	1.1–4.8	15–60	6–12		
Ethanol: ton of crop required to give 1 ton of ethanol.											
Equivalent mean	18.9	15	8.5	8.5	4.1	3.6	4.3	18.9	3.1	2.2	4.3
range	14–30	12–17	6–11	7–14	3.6–4.4		3.5–4.8	14–30	2.7–3.8		3.5–6.0
Ethanol: litres of ethanol produced by 1 ton of crop.											
Equivalent mean	70	100	170	130	300	350	300	70	400	580	290
range	60–75	70–110	160–180		270–350				–		220–320

	1	2	3	4	5	6	7	8	9	10	11
Ethanol: ton ethanol/ha/a Equivalent mean	4.7	3.3	1.2	1.76	0.7	0.71	0.4	2.0	2.4		
range	3–9.5	1.8–6.2	1–6	0.8–3.5	0.2–1.5	0.4–1.5	0.2–0.9	1–4	2–4		
Ethanol: litres/ha/a Equivalent mean	6000	4200	1600	2000	900	900	500	2500	3000		
range	3800–12000	2300–7800	500–4000	1000–4400	250–2000	500–1900	250–1200	1000–5000	2000–5000		
Carbohydrate content % mean	Sucrose 15	Sucrose 17	Starch 28	Starch 28	Starch 59	Starch 67	Starch 56	Sucrose 15	Starch 74	Starch 100	Sucrose 50
range	12–17	14–20	25–32	16–30	55–67		50–70	12–17	60–85		42–60

Ethanol based chemical product	t ethanol required per ton of product
Ethylene	1.71
LDPE	1.77
Acetaldehyde	1.16
Acetic acid	0.89
Acetic anhydride	0.92
Ethyl acetate	1.22
VCM	0.781
PVC	0.78
Butadiene	2.47

Source: Humphreys and Glasgow Ltd., 1980.

[1] This does *not* imply that a crop takes one year to grow and that it may be cropped throughout the year, but only that the land will give these approximate yields at an average annual rate.

[2] Grain sorghum figures based on dry weight basis (i.e. *not* as cropped).

[3] Average growing period 120 days so possibility of double cropping exists.

[4] Not a crop as such, but extracted from starch crops.

[5] Not strictly a crop but a by-product from cane or beet after removal of 'sugar' for conventional sugar production.

Table 2.3 Raw materials for alcohol production

Raw materials	Composition (%) of natural or fresh material		Growth cycle (months)	Agricultural productivity t/ha (average Brazil)	Alcohol production		
	Sugars[1]	Starch			Basic steps	Average yield	
						litre/ton	litre/ha
Sugarcane (stalk)	13–17		18	50	Grinding Fermentation Distillation	67	3350
Sorghum Stalk	12–17		4	35		70	2450/4900[2]
Grain	1–2	55–70		3	Distillation	340	1020/2040[2]
Stalk and grain						410	3470/6940[2]
Manioc (roots)	2–5	25–35	22	12.5	Disintegration Cooking Saccharification Fermentation Distillation	180	
Babassu (coconut)		12–16	84–96	2.5		80	200

Source: Ribeiro Filho, 1979.
[1] As Glucose.
[2] Estimated production considering one/two crops per year, respectively.

between 15–18 hours. A further advantage is that sugarcane cultivation does not result in soil erosion problems; continuous sugarcane production extending over several centuries has been recorded in a number of locations including Brazil, without major deleterious effects.

The negative aspects are that it requires good land and an abundance of water. Its yield must be over 40 tonne/ha to be industrially and financially viable; it ferments rapidly after cutting; the process technology is not fully developed and in Brazil its productivity is still low compared with other parts of the world. Although a large amount of potentially cultivatable land is available, the tendency exists to expand sugarcane production into already used agricultural areas, thus competing with its food production potential.

A further constraint is that many traditional sugar factories operate for relatively short seasons—around 6 months—because of unsuitable seasons which reduce the content of crystallizable sucrose.

An enormous variety of products can be obtained from sugar. Juice and bagasse are the starting points, from which many industrial processes can be developed (see Fig. 2.2).

Brazilian sugarcane production is currently approximately 100 million tonnes annually, from a cultivated area of over 2.5 million ha 20% of which is for alcohol production. Figure 2.3 shows the occurrence of sugarcane in Brazil; the centre-south region is the most important area, followed by the north north-east.

2   Sorghum (Sorghum vulgare) (Fig. 2.4)

Of the family Graminae, sorghum is one of the earliest known plants to have been cultivated and one of the world's most important crops. It is used for food, stock feed, forage, hay, silage, syrup, sugar and for making paper, industrial alcohol, whisky, beer etc. It can be grown in poor soils, but requires warm soil for germination and hot weather for growth. Its vegetative cycle is only 4 months which allows for two crops a year. Sorghum plants exhaust the soil considerably, they dry it out and deplete it, particularly of nitrates and also require frequent land preparation.

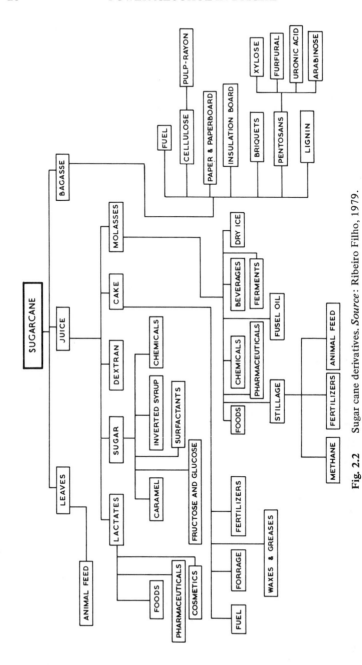

Fig. 2.2   Sugar cane derivatives. *Source*: Ribeiro Filho, 1979.

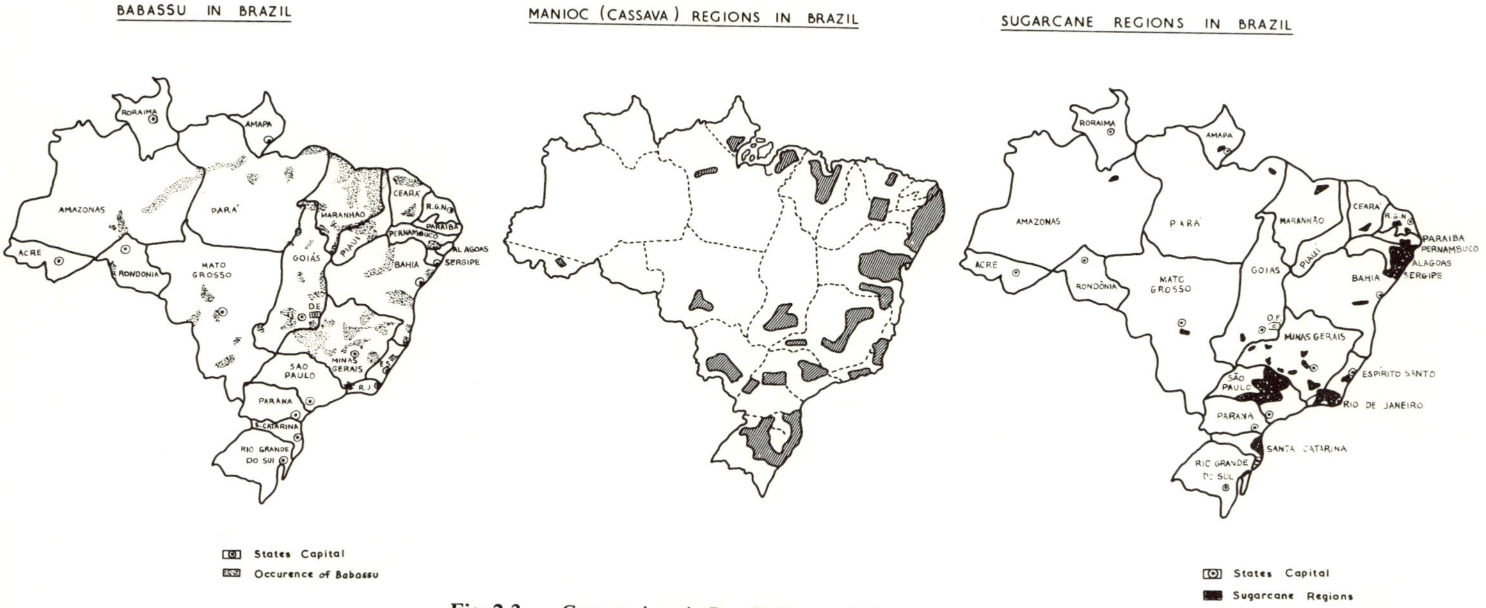

BABASSU IN BRAZIL

MANIOC (CASSAVA) REGIONS IN BRAZIL

SUGARCANE REGIONS IN BRAZIL

States Capital
Occurence of Babassu

States Capital
Sugarcane Regions

Fig. 2.3 Crop regions in Brazil. *Source:* Bôto Dantas, 1980.

Although it was introduced in Brazil some 40 years ago, Brazil has no industrial experience with sorghum. But recently it has received greater attention as a potential source for producing alcohol, partly because its juice can be extracted and fermented using the same equipment as for sugarcane. It represents a good additional crop to sugarcane offering better utilization of installed capacity of distilleries that previously used sugar only.

3   Cassava or Manioc (Manihot esculanta) (Fig. 2.4) (Maura Leitâo, 1979)

A member of the spurge family (*Euphorbiacae*) it is also known as mandioca, yuca and tapioca. Cassava (one of the world's greatest root crops) is a shrubby perennial, about 9 feet (2.5 metres) high, with deeply lobed leaves. Its roots (the source of starch) are quite large—some 3 feet (1 metre) each and a total weight of more than 20 lb. (9 kg) per plant. There are many varieties.

It is very tolerant of adverse growing conditions, but cannot withstand frost, growth stops at temperatures below 10–13°C. It is better adapted to the regions between the 15° parallels; at altitudes above 100m growth becomes slow; it requires 1000–1500mm of well distributed rainfall per year, but can withstand long periods of drought. The growth period may be as short as 6–7 months and as long as 24 months (22 months in Brazil), though the roots tend to become fibrous and less palatable after twelve months; yields of between 14–20 tonnes/ha are obtained and a tonne of roots can yield about 170 litres of alcohol. There are 200 different varieties of cassava in Brazil and the government is currently selecting five of these, which have a high carbohydrate content, for detailed study. Cassava contains about 30% fermentable carbohydrate. Table 2.4 shows the composition of cassava roots. Brazilian production is the largest in the world—some 30 million tonnes yearly grown on 2 million ha. It is a major source of food.

Brazil has experience of production in a plant operating at Divinopolis (MG) from 1932–1942, which at one time produced 0.6 million litres/year. Currently Petrobrás is operating

Table 2.4   Composition of cassava roots

Component	g/100g of dry matter
Starch	80-89
Total sugars	3.6-6.2
Reducing sugars	0.1-2.8
Pentosans	0.1-1.1
Fibre	1.7-3.8
Protein	2.1-6.2
Fat	0.2-0.7
Ash	0.9-2.4

Source: Barretts de Menezes, 1982.

an alcohol distillery at Curvelo (MG) with a capacity of 60000 litres per day—presently a new distillery is being installed in the North of Parana to produce another 60000 litres per day.

The major disadvantages of cassava, compared with sugarcane, include: the need to be re-planted annually; difficulties for mechanization, particularly harvesting; land to be ploughed and planted after each crop; higher industrial cost; it requires more sophisticated technology and consumes more electricity and combustibles, for more of its energy must come from external sources. The bagasse can provide only 25% of the fuel needed to run a cassava mill. It must be processed soon after harvesting (though if slicing or flaking with a drying process is added, it can be stored for long periods). It poses more serious erosion problems. In 1980 some 0.7 million ha would have been planted involving some 65000 farm workers, by 1990 about 730000 families, by the year 2000 some 18 million ha and 1.4 million families could be involved in cassava production. On the other hand Carioca *et al*. (1981) argue that cassava is a strong alternative alcohol crop since: it can be grown on marginal and presently unused lands; it requires less water; it provides four times more job opportunities than sugarcane cultivation; it is much less dependent on world market price fluctuations; its use could help to reduce regional disparities.

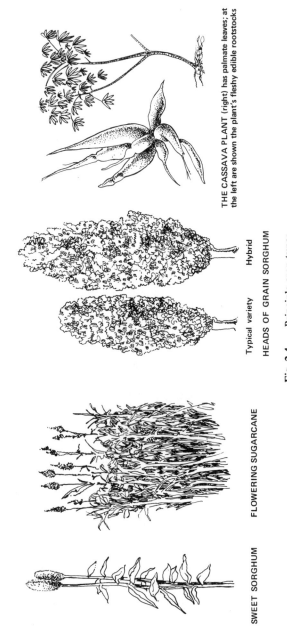

THE CASSAVA PLANT (right) has palmate leaves; at the left are shown the plant's fleshy edible rootstocks

Hybrid

Typical variety

HEADS OF GRAIN SORGHUM

FLOWERING SUGARCANE

SWEET SORGHUM

Fig. 2.4   Principle crop types.

Its economic feasibility, in the present circumstances, depends largely on the marketing of several by-products. But if more financial and technical assistance is given to many small producers productivity could improve significantly. (Figures 2.3 and 2.5 show cassava producing regions and cassava products.)

4 Babassu (Orbignya species) (Ribeiro Filho, 1979)

It is a tall palm with feathery leaves that grows wild in tropical North-Eastern Brazil. The kernels of its hard shelled nuts (see Fig. 2.6) are the source of babassu oil, similar in properties and uses to coconut oil.

The babassu nut is one of the most promising alternative energy sources. It has been known since the nineteenth century and there are several species including the 'attalea' family. It is roughly estimated that productivity is up to 3 tons/ha and Brazil's crop area is 15 million ha. The state of Maranhao produces 75% of the crop (see Fig. 2.3).

Fructification commences between the seventh and eighth year and it produces from 3–6 clusters/year, each containing between 150–300 'coconuts'. Its productive life is estimated at between 10–35 years. The babassu coconut is constituted of three layers: the middle layer or mesocarp (23% of the coconut as an average) contains the bulk of the starch, which makes up about 15–16% of the coconut and is the raw material for ethanol fermentation. Figure 2.7 shows the wide range of by-products that can be obtained using babassu as a starting point.

5 Various (Bôto Dantas, 1979)

The number of plant species which are being investigated as possible sources of hydrocarbon fuels and chemical feedstocks continues to grow. Brazil has identified as many as fifty other different plants, crops etc. as probable future sources of ethanol. Many vegetables are investigated as a source of oil. Brazil has 20% of the world's forest resources and their lumber industry creates over 15 million tons of 'green junk' and residues that could produce, if fully utilized,

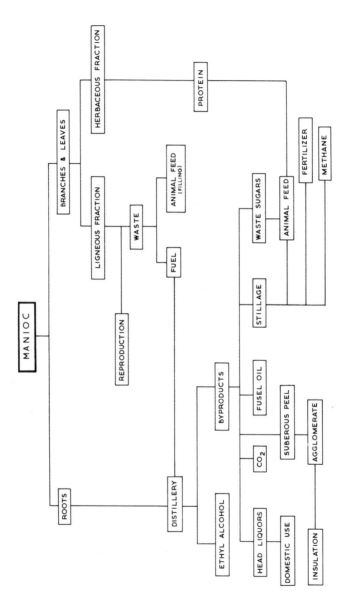

Fig. 2.5   Products from the whole processing of manioc. *Source*: Ribeiro Filho, 1979.

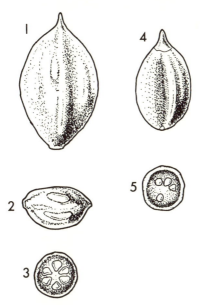

Fig. 2.6   The babassu nut. *Orbignya oleifera*: (1) the whole nut; (2) vertical section; (3) horizontal section. *Orbignya martiana*: (4) whole fruit; (5) horizontal sections. (*Source*: T. J. Barretts de Menezes, 1982.)

approximately 4×10^9 litres of ethanol plus 3 million tons of charcoal.

Other plants of great potential include the Marmoleiro Preto (*Croton sonderianus*) capable of producing between 400–2000 litres of ethanol per ha which with extensive cultivation could employ a million persons and produce 10×10^9 litres of ethanol. Other plants mentioned are the *Euphorbia tirmcalli, E. athyris, E. actea, E. resinifera*, the rubber tree *Hevea sp.* among others. Of particular interest is the *Euphorbia tirmcalli* tree which can produce significant quantities of a milk-like emulsion of hydrocarbon in water, an acre of mature trees might be able to produce 25 barrels of fuel per year.

In the United States corn has been considered as a raw material for ethanol production. Brazil on the other hand has not seriously considered using corn, although 14 million ha/a are grown. This is because corn is a staple food, and in any

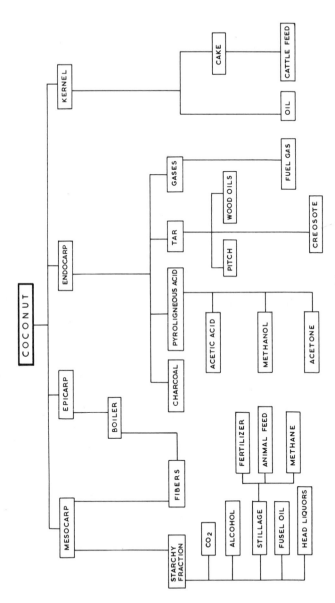

Fig. 2.7 Products from the whole processing of babassu. *Source:* Ribeiro Filho, 1979.

case Brazilian yields at 1.2 t/ha/a are only a quarter of those obtained in the US.

Barretts de Menezes (1982) has recently reported the Brazilian production, yields and programmes for producing ethanol from sugarcane, cassava, babassu and other starchy crops (see Tables 2.5 and 2.6). He believes that Brazil should have a policy for diversifying its alcohol crops. This would first increase the level of crop protection, since genetically homogeneous populations are especially vulnerable to disease and pests, and secondly could minimize the socio-economic disadvantages associated with monocultures.

Table 2.5   Production and yield of starchy materials in Brazil

Carbohydrate source	Annual production $\times 10^6$ t	Productivity t/ha/year raw material	Ethanol yield	
			raw mat. l/t	Area l/h/year
Cassava	26	12	180	2160
Sweet potato	1.0	9	125	1125
Corn	14	12	385	462
Babassu nut	12.4	3.0	80	240

Source: Barretts de Menezes, 1982.

Table 2.6   Programme for the production of alcohol; raw materials up to January 1981

Raw materials	Number of projects	Annual Production $(10^3 m^3)$
Sugarcane (annexed)	172	4522.7
Sugarcane (independent)	158	4086.7
Cassava	12	271.5
Babassu nut	1	9.0
Sweet sorghum	1	3.0
Total	344	8892.9

Source: Barretts de Menezes, 1982.

References

Anon. (1980), 'Opportunities for a biosolar economy in Brazil and its challenges to the developing world', *Biomass Digest,* **2** (2), 117.

Anon. (1977), *I Simposio Sabre Produçao de Alcool Do Noreste,* Fortaleza, 10-12 August.

Barretts de Menezes, T. J. (1982), 'Starchy materials for alcohol fuel production', *Process Biochemistry,* **17** (3), 32-5.

Benemann, R. J. (1980), 'The Brazilian alcohol programme', *Biosources Digest,* **21** (3), 156-79.

Bôto Dantas, R. (1979), 'Alcool e otras fontes alternativas de energia como substitutivas de petroleo' (pt. 1), *Brasil Açúcareiro,* **94** (4), 22-37.

Bôto Dantas, R. (1980), 'Production of alcohol: the Brazilian experience', *International Sweetner Alcohol Conference. The Future of Sugar,* April, London.

British Chamber of Commerce in Brazil (1980), *Information Circular* No. 18, September.

Brown, L. (1980), *Food or Fuel: New Competition for the World's Cropland,* World Watch Institute, Paper 35, Washington DC.

Calvin, M. (1980), 'The power that grows on trees', *The Guardian,* 20 November, London.

Carioca, M. *et al.* (1981), 'Technological and socio-economic aspects of cassava-based autonomous mini distilleries in Brazil', *Biomass,* **1,** 99-114.

Coombs, J. and Parker, K. J. (1979), 'Biomass future developments', *Biomass for Energy Conference (C-20),* Royal Society, July, London.

FAST (1979), 'Sub-programme C—Bio-society', Commission of the European Communities, DG XII, FAST/ACPM/79/14-3E, Brussels.

Goldstein, L. *et al.* (1980), 'Fermentation ethanol as a petroleum substitute', *15th Intersociety Energy Conversion Engineering Conference (IECEC 80),* 18-11 August, Seattle, Washington, USA.

Goodman, N. and Pimentel, D. (1979), 'Energy conversion as an alternative energy source', *Science/Land Utilization,* **20** (1), 28-31.

Hall, D. O. (1979), 'World Biomass, an overview', *Biomass for Energy Conference (C-20),* Royal Society, July.

Hammond, A. (1979), 'Biomass conversion, a rediscovered source of fuels', *Development Digest,* **17** (3), 4-11.

Humphreys and Glasgow Ltd (1980), 'Agrosources Chemical', personal communication, 22 Carlisle Place, London SW1.

Lyons, T. P. (1982), *Gasohol: A Step to Energy Independence,* Chapman and Hall Ltd, Andover, UK.

Macrae, N. (1979), 'Oh Brazil (A survey)', *The Economist*, **272** (7092), 20-1.

Maura Leitâo, D. (1979), 'Etanol como fonte de energia', *Brasil Açúcareiro*, **93** (1).

Mouth, T. H. (1979), 'Unlike money, diesel fuel grows on trees', *Science*, **206** (4417), 46.

Oliveira, H. P. (1979), 'Alcool carburante', *Brazil Açúrareiro*, **94** (4).

Ribeiro Filho, F. A. (1979), 'The ethanol based chemical industry in Brazil', *UNIDO Workshop on Fermentation Alcohol, 26-30 March*, Doc. ID/WG 3 93/4, UNIDO, Vienna.

Truda, L. (1971), *A Defesa de Produçâo Açúcareira*, Instituto do Açúcar e do Álcool (IAA), Rio de Janeiro.

US Department of Commerce (1977), 'Alternative energy technologies in Brazil', *Technical Information Service (P13-297860)*, February, Washington DC.

Yates, R. A (1980), 'Alternative renewable raw materials for alcohol production'. *International Sweetner Alcohol Conference. The Future of Sugar*, April, London.

3 THE NATIONAL ALCOHOL PROGRAMME (PNA) AND ITS ENERGY OBJECTIVES

Faced with an acute oil import dependence and stimulated by a sharp fall in sugar prices in the international market, the Brazilian Government finally launched the National Alcohol Programme (PNA), created by Decree No. 76.593, on 14 November 1975.

It should be clearly stated, however, that the PNA defined by the Brazilian Government for the purpose of substituting fuel derived from petroleum with ethanol is only one of various alternatives considered by the government departments in the effort to attenuate the situation of dependence which Brazil faces with regard to energy. Besides the necessary measures taken for locating and exploiting new petroleum producing areas, other sources of energy are under deeper and systematic study, such as hydro-electricity, coal, wood, bagasse, shale oil etc., which Brazil has in abundance. The PNA as defined by the Govenment in 1975 is, therefore, only one of several options being considered to contribute to the solution of the overall problem and should not be discussed and examined solely from the restricted standpoint of its economic feasibility.

The programme implementation was a political one, and economic and technical factors played secondary roles. Energy dependence and currency savings were key factors.

3.1 Energy Goals (Gochnarg, 1979)

As noted previously, Brazil is the Third World's most petroleum-dependent country and also possesses the highest external debt. To remedy this foreign dependence, the Government has planned an energy policy—assuming an annual growth rate of 8% on the GNP for the period 1979–1987, whose main objectives are:

1 Intensify the primary sources most abundant in Brazil;
2 To try to increase available resources;
3 To rationalize both consumption and production of energy;
4 To reduce dependence on imported petroleum, the main source of the primary energy.

The highlights of these objectives are:

Ethanol
— Substitution of ethanol for gasoline;
— Substitution of ethanol for diesel oil;
— Increasing ethanol production capacity aiming at reducing oil imports;
— A secondary role in chemical feedstock substitution.

Petroleum
— To intensify exploration activities in the country and abroad particularly offshore on the Brazilian continental shelf—where Petrobrás (the national petroleum company) has achieved good results and where many 'risk contracts' (the Government takes shares in any profits but does not incur any losses) have been signed with foreign oil companies.

Hydroelectricity
— All economically feasible hydraulic potential will continue to be exploited in preference to other primary sources. It is a non-depletable source of energy, and also given the hydroelectric potential of Brazil, the second most important source of energy.

Uranium
— Policies are less clear, but primarily to implement uranium use as an alternative source of energy (light water reactor; some 70000 nuclear megawatts by the year 2000).

Coal
— New policies to encourage the use of coal and as a result increase production in spite of low quality.

Shale Oil
— Work will continue in several fields of research aiming at

the economic exploitation of the most abundant source of energy in the nation.

Bagasse/Firewood/Others

– The traditional and important sources of energy for the Brazilians, albeit with downward trends. Solar energy, wind and tidal energy are also under study, as are vegetable oils, which are seen to be promising.

3.2 The National Energy Balance

The consumption of energy *per capita* in Brazil is still low by the standards of many developed countries, e.g. one-tenth of that of the US. None the less with present industrial development growth and with an expected population of 218 million people, if present trends continue, by the year 2000 energy consumption will increase at least five-fold. Petroleum is estimated to account for 70% of total energy consumption i.e. some 5 million barrels per day. With the implementation of the automobile industry in Brazil in the early 1950s, petrol consumption increased from circa 10% of the total energy consumption in 1940 to 44% in 1973 and stabilizing at 45% in 1979.

Because the automobile fleet is growing rapidly, the gasohol programme will hardly be able to meet this rapid increase in the automobile fuel requirements. Figure 3.1 gives an idea of the trends between 1957 and 1979.

According to the Ministry of Mines and Energy's National Energy Balance Projections, by 1987 petrol will account for 34.2% of the total primary energy consumption, equivalent to 64.5 million tons; as opposed to just 2.1% expected from ethanol contribution, although some 'alcohol optimist' put it higher to 7% of the total petroleum consumption in 1985.

Table 3.1 shows the primary usage consumption from different sources of energy between 1967 and 1987 (see also Fig. 3.2).

Forecast estimates are based on an estimated 8% annual growth of GNP from 1979 to 1987 (growth for 1981 has been set at 5%). Only shale oil with 1.2% and charcoal with 1.9% and natural gas with 0.7% are expected to contribute less than alcohol energy to overall requirements. Even the

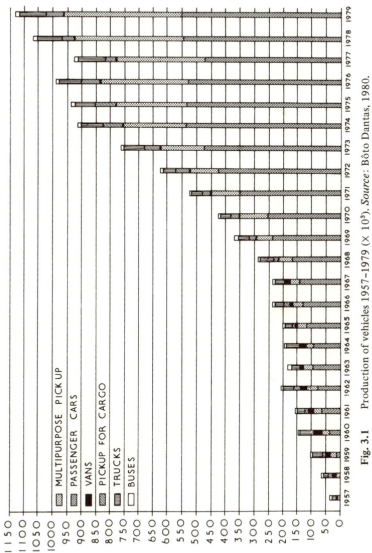

Fig. 3.1   Production of vehicles 1957–1979 ($\times$ 10^3). *Source:* Bôto Dantas, 1980.

Table 3.1

Source: Gochnarg, 1979.
*1 tpe (tons of petroleum equivalent) = 12.4 × 10⁹J.

Primary energy consumption in tons of petroleum equivalent

Year	Petroleum		Natural Gas		Alcohol		Shale Oil		Subtotal		Water Power		Coal		Firewood		Bagasse		Charcoal		Uranium		Total	
	10^3 tpe*	%	10^3 tpe	%	10^3 tpe	%	10^3 tpe	%	10^3 tpe	%	10^3 tpe	%	10^3 tpe	%	10^3 tpe	%	10^3 tpe	%	10^3 tpe	%	10^3 tpe	%	10^3 tpe	%
1967	17371	33.8	105	0.2	367	0.7	—		17813	34.7	8465	16.5	2048	4.0	19291	37.4	2825	5.5	1003	1.0	—		51475	100.0
1968	20270	37.9	93	0.2	160	0.3	—		20532	38.4	8860	16.6	2317	4.3	18048	33.8	2564	4.8	1094	2.1	—		53415	100.0
1969	21993	33.7	96	0.2	27	0.0	—		22116	38.9	9481	16.7	2342	4.0	18999	33.4	2762	4.9	1191	2.1	—		56891	100.0
1970	23311	38.1	104	0.2	156	0.2	—		23570	38.5	11560	18.9	2391	3.9	18809	30.8	3356	5.5	1484	2.4	—		61170	100.0
1971	26186	39.9	140	0.2	213	0.3	—		26539	40.4	12549	19.1	2431	3.8	18862	28.8	3559	5.4	1655	2.5	—		65595	100.0
1972	26740	41.0	166	0.2	328	0.4	—		29234	41.6	14918	21.3	2491	3.6	17661	25.2	3990	5.7	1822	2.6	—		70116	100.0
1973	34240	43.9	178	0.2	260	0.3	—		34678	44.4	17055	21.9	2493	3.2	17429	22.4	4459	5.7	1897	2.4	—		78011	100.0
1974	36947	43.8	339	0.4	160	0.2	—		37446	44.4	19011	22.5	2469	2.9	18511	20.0	4361	5.2	2536	3.0	—		84364	100.0
1975	30300	43.5	369	0.4	136	0.1	—		39805	44.0	21412	23.7	2850	3.2	19328	21.4	4032	4.5	2897	3.2	—		90324	100.0
1976	42894	43.3	367	0.4	144	0.1	—		43405	43.8	23626	23.8	3435	3.5	21294	21.5	4166	4.2	3154	3.2	—		99080	100.0
1977	43063	41.7	505	0.5	537	0.5	—		44105	42.7	26953	26.1	4106	4.0	20885	20.2	4714	4.6	2489	2.4	—		103252	100.0

Primary energy consumption forecast in tons petroleum equivalent

Year	Petroleum		Natural Gas		Alcohol		Shale Oil		Subtotal		Water Power		Coal		Firewood		Bagasse		Charcoal		Uranium		Total	
1978	46452	42.4	614	0.6	1461	1.3	—		48527	44.3	28088	25.6	4830	4.4	20676	18.8	5058	4.6	2554	2.3	—		109733	100.0
1979	49297	42.5	659	0.6	1967	1.6	—		51923	44.7	30934	26.5	4793	4.1	20469	17.5	5602	4.8	2655	2.3	137	0.1	116513	100.0
1980	50269	40.6	677	0.6	2479	2.0	—		53425	43.2	34066	27.5	5736	4.6	20065	16.4	6168	5.0	2939	2.4	1114	0.9	123713	100.0
1981	51180	39.0	736	0.6	2521	1.9	—		54437	41.5	39886	30.3	6172	4.7	20062	15.3	6600	5.0	3086	2.3	1114	0.9	131357	100.0
1982	51823	37.2	976	0.7	2598	1.9	—		55397	39.8	45069	32.3	7878	5.6	19861	14.2	7013	5.0	3152	2.3	1114	0.8	139474	100.0
1983	54461	36.8	1109	0.8	3001	2.0	—		58571	39.6	49410	33.3	8496	5.7	19663	13.3	7634	5.1	3284	2.2	1114	0.8	148002	100.0
1984	56069	35.6	1142	0.7	3357	2.1	1154	0.7	61722	39.1	53252	33.9	8886	5.7	19466	12.4	8023	5.1	3481	2.2	2412	1.6	157242	100.0
1985	58478	35.0	1172	0.7	3541	2.1	1154	0.7	64345	38.5	57816	34.6	10004	6.0	19272	11.6	8405	5.0	3600	2.2	3517	2.1	166959	100.0
1986	61288	34.6	1218	0.7	3735	2.1	1732	1.0	67973	38.4	61626	34.7	10647	6.0	19079	10.8	8805	5.0	3600	2.0	5545	3.1	177275	100.0
1987	64477	34.2	1268	0.7	3941	2.1	2310	1.2	71996	38.2	65516	34.8	11244	6.0	18888	10.0	9224	4.9	3600	1.9	7761	4.2	188229	100.0

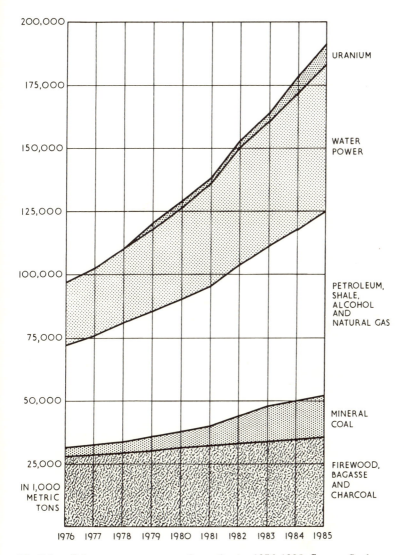

Fig. 3.2   Primary energy consumption estimates 1976–1985. *Source*: Coulson-Thomas, 1980.

contribution of firewood is expected to account for 10%. Of the 3.5 million tons petrol equivalent of alcohol production expected in 1985, 73% of alcohol will be utilized as fuel alcohol and just 20% will be channelled to the chemical industry—some 1.5×10^9 litres depending on the sources.

The average annual growth rates of primary energy consumption during 1967–1977 were 6.7% for primary energy; 6.8% in the case of petroleum and 12.6% for alcohol, which is the fastest growing sector. Doubt remains nevertheless as to whether, in any high-*per-capita*-energy consumption society, alcohol would provide the solution, even in countries with the biomass potential of Brazil.

3.3 Institutions linked to the National Alcohol Programme (PNA) (Maura Leitâo, 1979; Petrobrás, 1980)

The PNA is an interrelated and overlapping programme whose influence is felt in many official organizations.

3.3.1 *Commissão Nacional de Energia (CNE)—National Energy Commission*

This is a transitory institution, created to programme policies and to establish standards and guidelines in the energy field. It also examines conservation measures, increase in domestic oil production, and the substitution of petroleum by other forms of energy. It is directly subordinated to the Presidency of the Republic, and is headed by the Vice-President of Brazil. However, many other Ministries and official organizations take part in the CNE.

3.3.2 *Conselho Nacional do Álcool (CNAL)—National Alcohol Council*

This was formed at the same time as the PNA, and headed by the Ministry of Industry and Commerce (MIC), but it is integrated by the General Secretaries of eight Ministries. This was the outcome of the Second National Development Plan (II–PND). Within the PNA the CNAL is in charge of identifying the participation of the several departments associated

with the PNA defining the criteria for new unit location,
viz:

- establishing the annual production programme for the
  various types of alcohol;
- deciding about modernization, enlargement, or installation proposals of alcohol plants;
- tying up credit lines, elaborating general standards for
  commercialization prices;
- examining, following up and approving Proálcool-related
  activities carried out by public administration institutions;
- authorizing exports of residual syrup and/or any other
  type of alcohol.

The approval of a given project by the CNAL requires the
previous clearance of the *Commissão Executiva Nacional do
Álcool* (CENAL).

3.3.3 *Commissão Executiva Nacional do Álcool (CENAL) —National Executive Alcohol Commission*

It is presided over by the Secretary General of the MIC,
composed of the head executives of the IAA (see below), the
Secretariat of Industrial Technology (STI), the executive
Secretariat of the Industrial Development Council (CDI), and
the CNP. CENAL's basic tasks are to give technical and
administrative support to the CNAL and to co-ordinate the
execution of Proálcool. Its main objectives include:

- to give technical and administrative support to CNAL,
  through its institutions;
- to analyse alcohol distillery projects for modernization,
  expansion and engineering and decide on adequacy to
  proalcool;
- to examine and decide on the approval of propositions
  related to Proálcool submitted by public and private
  institutions;
- to follow up public corporations' proalcool related
  activities;
- to promote and co-ordinate studies, research and development of interest to the Proálcool;

— to make a monthly report of its activities to be sent to CNAL.

3.3.4 *Instituto do Açúcar e do Álcool (IAA)—The Sugar and Alcohol Institute*

The main activities of the IAA, after Decree No. 82.476 of 23 October 1978 can be summarized as:

— keeping records of all alcohol distilleries registered in Brazil, regardless of its raw materials;
— establishing the basic price and the technical specifications for the residual syrup and for non-fuel uses;
— establishing the parity between alcohol and sugar— parity prices based on 42 litres of alcohol for 60 kg of sugar standard—with the approval of the Ministry of Mines and Energy;
— analysing sugarcane alcohol production projects.

3.3.5 *Conselho Nacional do Petróleo (CNP)—National Petroleum Council*

Its main tasks and goals are as follows:

— guaranteeing the purchase of the country's entire alcohol production, at prices established by the IAA from affiliated distilleries;
— scheduling alcohol distribution, from producing sources of consuming companies and to oil distributors;
— establishing blending sites;
— proposing to the CNAL the prices of alcohol for fuel uses;
— managing the resources guaranteed by the commercialization of fuel alcohol aiming to improve the production technology and the utilization of fuel alcohol as well as Research and Development and technical assistance to raw material production;
— ensuring an appropriate alcohol price per litre—for the chemical industry—equivalent to 35% of the ethylene kg price as established by government institutions.

4 Policies (Almeida, 1979; Gonzaga Bertelli, 1980)

Unlike earlier approaches, in this new phase, alcohol production should develop gradually into an independent venture in many locations based on both sugar and starch containing feedstocks. This departure from the traditional by-product status of alcohol to one as a major product should bring about important economic, social, political and technological repercussions in Brazil.

The Government supports Proálcool in the following ways:

— market guarantee for all ethanol produced;
— administered price of ethanol pegged to gasoline price at the gas station;
— subsidized loans for implementation of agricultural base and alcohol distilleries.

Other objectives include:
—Private participation, diversification of financial assistance, for future development of the domestic alcohol technology; priority for projects for developing alternative feedstocks, other than sugarcane; diversification of equipment production; introduction of training programmes at secondary and higher education levels to produce the necessary manpower; higher efficiency through better utilization of technology and materials; minimization of the cost of structural changes; improved regional imbalances in alcohol production and transport costs etc.

Apart from its important role as fuel, another objective is that ethanol should play a significant role as a chemical feedstock, despite being relegated to a secondary role by the PNA (at least in the short term). Industrial alcohol not going to the fuel market is currently being used as a solvent and as a cleansing agent, in the pharmaceutical and cosmetic industry, and, of course, as feedstock in the chemical industry where its consumption is expected to grow much more rapidly than in any other traditional uses of alcohol. The potential use of ethanol as a chemical feedstock, particularly looking to the substitution of imported petrochemicals, is quite large in spite of not being fully organized by the PNA. Ethanol is also beginning to be utilized as an energy source for heavy industry and even for the production of gas on an industrial scale. This is the case of the *Companhia de Gas* (Comgas) in São Paulo, although it is still in very early stages of development.

Improvements in both industrial and agricultural technologies will require intense research and development and managerial efforts—and in the case of agriculture important structural changes. They promise to strengthen the base of the capital goods industrial sector. For example, the proliferation of distilleries is expected to stimulate that sector by adding a major new internal market. The distillery-based industrial capital sector is already booming. In the long term it is expected to develop a complete chemical industry based on ethanol rather than petroleum. It should be noted that whatever the outcome, petroleum will remain an important source in spite of alcohol's potential.

The programme's expected economic objectives should include savings in some foreign exchange through substitution of imported fossil fuel and strengthening on the internal market through a more intensified use of domestic production factors. At the same time, however, more clear policies need to be followed if the challenge and objectives are to be met and achieved. Such policies might include, as Gonzaga Bertelli suggests, the following:

1 adequate and realistic prices for alcohol in order to attract capital—domestic or foreign on more favourable terms;
2 an independent price, not linked to sugar, to avoid uncertainty in the alcohol industry;
3 tax incentives to investors;
4 government should guarantee a market for alcohol;
5 greater efficiency and simplification of sources for approval of new projects;
6 more finance to be available; the agencies involved in the PNA should be incorporated within the national banking systems;
7 centralization of all responsibilities, within one agency, to study new projects;
8 more resources to be allocated for R&D on ethanol rather than dispersion in many alternative sources, since in the

short term at least, alcohol is the most practical and viable;

9 replanning alcohol production objectives.

Critics of the PNA have emphasized that planning should be done on a more realistic basis, taking into consideration the different conditions in different parts of the country. The PNA planners should pay greater attention to: the relationship between investment and productive capacity; better technical and economic utilization of raw materials; equipment and materials which result in the optimization of agriculture and industrial processes; better utilization of infrastructure necessary for the production and utilization of alcohol.

Some of these deficiencies were recognized by the government when there was a crisis of confidence in the whole plan and some of the original objectives had to be rectified. As a result Decree No. 83.700 of July 1979 gave a new role to the IAA to examine new projects for modernization, expansion and installation of alcohol distilleries and their functions according to Proálcool objectives; to analyse new proposals of public sectors, concerned with the PNA; to take greater advantage of the development of the public sector activities related to the PNA and to promote and co-ordinate the implementation of industries associated with such programmes.

The many achievements of the PNA, combined with the downturn of sugar prices and the continuing high costs of petroleum, appear likely to ensure the implementation of many of the PNA objectives. Nevertheless, the PNA according to some commentators (e.g. Drevon and Thery, 1977) leaves many things to be desired, particularly in social terms, since it is far from complying with original objectives of reducing social inequalities and is in the main endorsing the opposite.

3.4.1 *The PNA 1975, Its Major Implications and Challenges*

If the PNA is successful, as it seems so far, Brazil should become more self-sufficient in both energy and technology in addition to benefits from economic, social and political improvements if proper policies are pursued. Agriculture in particular could form the basis for supplying Brazil's needs, not only for food, fibre and feed, but also for chemical feed-stocks and energy to a certain extent, because of the favourable combination of land area, latitude, population and stage of development.

But the PNA has to face many obstacles and it will require a considerable political support to overcome these. For example, if present energy growth rates continue some 30×10^9 litres of ethanol will be needed by 1985 to meet demand, and even if the projected PNA target is realized, ethanol will barely substitute for the annual demand increases between now and 1985; thus total petroleum imports will still continue to grow. The programme is not running as smoothly as predicted and, as things stand, only with great difficulty could such projections be met. For the 10.7×10^9 litre planned output by 1985 to be achieved on time, new distillery projects will be required with a combined capacity of 300000 litres per day. This calls for far more projects to be approved than are actually being approved. The upsurge in world sugar prices created a dilemma because in 1979 savings from the use of ethanol amounted to $300 million, whereas if the cane involved in producing alcohol had been utilized to make sugar, it would have fetched 1.5×10^9 at 1980 levels. During the previous 3 years Brazil's receipts for its sugar exports have on average paid for almost 35% of the imported crude oil during the same period. Therefore some economic experts are apprehensive that the PNA will lose impetus if world sugar prices continue to rise. They insist that to make the technological option irreversible and independent of the fluctuations of the international commodity market new distilleries should be built which operate directly from raw cane, by-passing sugar production and storage. By the end of 1979, for example, the IAA had approved the construction of eighty-seven such new 'autonomous' distilleries (autonomous distilleries are those not connected with sugar production or any other commodity). But at the same time it approved the construction of 139 standard distilleries which doubled the number of distilleries operating from sugar as an intermediary, leaving some doubts as to the earnestness of the government commitment to a fully independent alcohol programme.

Given the present difficulties with the balance of payments, there can be no guarantee that the government will not shift to sugar production again. It should be stressed that currently, due to the petroleum situation, greater emphasis is being given to alcohol production and, therefore, such a shift is unlikely unless important oil discoveries are made in the near future. Thus it has been suggested that the diversification of raw materials for alcohol production should be speeded up to rely less on sugar cane. On the other hand sugar refineries and alcohol distilleries are not run with the benefit of modern management techniques, nor do they use efficient technologies, and this must be considered, at present, the key institutional problem. The existence of an entrenched and protected interest group, that historically has not adopted new technologies or allowed competition, could well be an important stumbling block to the future of the PNA.

3.4.2 Technology (Lindeman and Rocchicciolo, 1979; Nicholson, 1979)

In the past decade quite important changes have taken place in Brazil in this field. The government is reluctant to see a continuing drain of foreign currency in the form of royalty payments, and royalties are therefore strictly limited to a maximum of 5% (in the case of the most sophisticated technology) the average level being about 3%; royalty payments are usually for a maximum of 5 years with the chief objective of gaining domestic control of foreign knowhow.

Today Brazil manufactures almost all its industrial equipment for the distilleries and is now able to offer for export its alcohol technology—including cultivation processes, machinery and equipment, sugar mills with annex distillation facilities, autonomous alcohol distilleries, gasohol knowhow, anhydrous and hydrated motor technology, hydrated alcohol pumps, storage tank manufacturing technology etc. By supporting alcohol production the PNA has helped the back-up industry—construction of equipment and distilleries is booming, which has allowed greater expansion and modernization of the domestic capital goods sector. The alcohol industry is now ready to produce over 150 distilleries/year with capacities ranging from $30m^3$/day to $240m^3$/day and even in the state of Mato Grosso do Sul there is a project for the construction of a 1.5 million litres/day plant. The major manufacturing companies include Mausa (*Metalúrgica de Acessorio para Usinas* S/A) Dedini S/A; CODISTIL (*Constructora de Destilarias Dedini* S/A) and ZANINI Company (an important exporter).

However, in the case of the sugarcane sector, the technology can be regarded, in general terms, as traditional and resistant to changes, although for the chemical sector there have been significant improvements. For example in 1974, 38% of the 3.8×10^9 (i.e. 1.44×10^9) total chemical sales was foreign owned, and plants being built (since early 1970s) contained 60–80% of imported components, but today imports often account for just 20% of equipment costs—mainly for instrumentation and special steel. None the less, foreign participation has been a fact of life in Brazil's manufacturing sector and the country remains highly dependent on foreign knowhow. For every dollar that Brazil spends on R&D it spends between 50 cents and $1 in buying foreign knowhow.

In 1978 alone Brazil spent $522.3 million on foreign technology and in the preceding 6 years 1.8×10^9—11% was for the chemical industry. This amount does not include 'indirect' transfer of knowhow which is much higher. Brazil spends only 0.3 to 0.6 of its GNP on R&D, a fact which should be borne in mind when considering Brazil's technological dependence. On the question of patents, of the approximately 3.5 million existing in the world, only 6% belong to the Third World and of this 6% between 90–95% are not being used at all in those nations. Brazil is no exception. However, interestingly enough, in a search for new ethanol patents in Brazil in the period 1977 up to 8 August 1980 (Ref. C4–17–5 DIAL CA. Search 77/80 V1. 9304.) of a total of thirty patents, twenty-one (70%) were found to be Brazilian. Furthermore, it appears that at least in the alcohol by-product technology, Brazil is making advances which may have important consequences for the development of their sucrochemical industry. At the same time, that is opening the doors of the 'alcohol age' to other countries and the PNA has played a central role. Currently, the state of the art of sucrochemistry can be regarded as a technology with ample room for improvements, particularly fermentation technology (see Table 4.4 and Fig. 4.4) where Brazil can learn much from foreign knowhow.

3.4.3 *Employment*

With a labour force estimated at about 40 million people, Brazil needs to create between 1.2 and 1.3 million new jobs a year. Employment creation is an important national priority and could be one of the most important social benefits of the PNA, particularly at the farm level.

Alcohol demand for energy crops will increase the land capable of cultivation for this purpose significantly. For example, to produce 4×10^9 litres of alcohol requires over 3 million ha of sugarcane employing 1 million of direct labour force—the national production target for 1985 is 10.7×10^9 litres. For cassava, to produce 2×10^9 litres of alcohol requires 1 million ha and 1.2 million workers in direct employment. The PNA requires the creation of 420000 new jobs (1980–1985) in the agricultural sector and another 42000 directly employed in the alcohol industry itself.

3.4.4 *Agriculture (Redfearn, 1980)*

The introduction of the PNA will have a tremendous impact in the agricultural sector. A threefold increase in alcohol production from 1979–1985 would not only require a large investment, it will also have serious implications for the whole agriculture sector. Yields which are low will not increase dramatically in the course of a few years, particularly in the most traditional areas, thus extensive land use may have to be the solution. Agriculture in some areas will need to be radically re-structured, but land ownership remains a very sensitive issue in Brazil.

After the failure of the Amazon Basin Programme the government is concentrating on the savannah, known locally as the 'Cerrados' an area covering some 180 million ha mainly in the centre of the country.

Previous attempts to open up the Cerrados has produced poor results, because the old soils have been leached of plant nutrients and aluminium concentrations are up to three times more than will be tolerated by most crops, although soil structure and climate are good.

Fortunately recent studies suggest that the aluminium and acidity problem can be solved by adding limestone— about 2 tons/ha depending upon crop, and fertility can be restored by adding about 150–180 kg of phosphate/ha and these maintained by adding nitrogen, phosphate, potassium, a trace of zinc, and good soil and crop management. The problem is that Brazil has to import most of the raw materials for its fertilizers. The PNA foresees an increased demand for fertilizers of 750000 tonnes per year if the production target is to be met by 1985. Thus the search must be for suitable nitrogen fixing crops which could be used in rotation. Currently attention is being given to modified soya strains, about 30% of the crop is inoculated with *Rhizobium*. Over 12 million ha of soya is grown.

In recent years progress has been made in increasing the yields of certain crops, for example, during the 1970s the average yield of sugarcane rose from 4300 kg/ha to 6000 kg/ha. There is a potential for further increases where the mechanization of agriculture remains low, although this has to balance against the rural unemployment that results from mechanization (Zanca, 1980).

3.4.5 *Financing (Bank of London and South America, 1979)*

Financing has been a serious problem for the PNA particularly due to the difficulties of raising money in the Brazilian domestic market, and because of bureaucratic delays. For example, in December 1978, of the distilleries approved by the CNAL 80 were refused finance and by mid-1979 of the 226 alcohol distillery projects approved only 133 were contracted after the *Banco do Brasil* (the major source of financing) had authorized their finance. Approval procedure is a source of delay, the time when the IAA proposes a new distillery and its acceptance by the CNAL is at least 3 months and often a whole year, and in the case of financing approval by the *Banco do Brasil*, the period is on average at least 1 year.

The new Proálcool financing conditions prevailing since mid-1979 include 12 years of amortization, plus a 3-year grace period. The outstanding balance of the loan is increased annually by an amount equal to 40% of the change in value of Brazilian Treasury bonds (ORTN). Interest charges vary from 2–6% per annum, depending on the type of distillery, raw materials and region of country (e.g. between 4–6% for dependent sugarcane distilleries; and 2% in the case of other feedstocks).

The financing limit is 80% of the fixed investment cost for sugarcane distilleries, and 90% of other feedstocks. Financing is available for, among other things; building, equipment, installation of equipment, laboratory facilities, office facilities, equipment feasibility studies, transport facilities, technical studies, project costs, acquisition of premises etc.

3.4.6 *Investment (Gochnarg, 1979)*

Capital investment required to distil huge quantities of alcohol is immense. A single oil refinery can produce an amount of petrol equivalent to the alcohol output of many distilleries (depending on capacity) and whilst all petroleum by-products are useful, for every litre of alcohol produced, there are 12–13 litres of effluent to be disposed of.

Estimates vary, but doubtless the PNA does require a high investment and, furthermore, there has been strong criticism of the way many projects were approved; many of these have been accepted at the preliminary stage only to run up later against technical objections. Economic analysis does not seem to be a factor in the investment, hence return on investment is wide ranging from 1.4% to 78% per annum. This together with financial difficulties created by mid-1979 a crisis of confidence in the whole PNA forcing the government to modify and replace some of its original objectives and to launch the second stage of PNA.

In addition to the 2 million ha land requirement for sugar-cane and cassava (0.35% of Brazil's territory) the cost of obtaining and preparing it for crop utilization may be as high as $600 million and the estimated required investment for these new facilities will be $1.1 $\times$ 10^9 in 1980 alone. To reach the 10.7 million m^3 year by 1985 investment by the government will be between $5-6 $\times$ 10^9. Official forecasts estimate a large cumulative expenditure totalling $10.4 $\times$ 10^9 by 1990 for the implementation of the alcohol industry and receptive structure for an annual consumption of 15–20 million m^3.

The 1980 proalcool budget provided Cr$22.34 $\times$ 10^9 for industrial distilleries, Cr$10 $\times$ 10^9 for agricultural distilleries, Cr$18 $\times$ 10^9 for agriculture and planting, Cr$2.68 $\times$ 10^9 for grants and Cr$1.89 $\times$ 10^9 for other expenses. The total allocated budget was Cr$54.9 $\times$ 10^9 ($1.094 $\times$ 10^9).

The average cost of one independent distillery facility with capacity for 150 m^3/180 days per year of sugarcane is between $11.5–15.5 million and for cassava between $15.5–17.0 million for 150 m^3/day over 330 days per year. The cassava distillery requires a fixed investment 20% higher than the equivalent independent sugarcane distillery because of the additional equipment needed for liquefication and saccharification. But the larger alcohol inventory necessary, due to alcohol legislation, entails a considerably higher working capital for sugarcane and as a result total investment differs only by about 10%.

3.4.7 *Foreign Exchange Savings*

Officially a considerable saving of foreign currency is expected from the PNA, although some critics question this. The blendings of ethanol and gasoline combined with changes in oil refinery operations may result in savings totalling by the end of 1980 some 50 million barrels annually.

The total expected foreign exchange savings for the first 11 years of the PNA is reckoned to be circa $4.44 $\times$ 10^9. These figures have been contested and other estimates are

$3-5 \times 10^9$ for the period 1977–1986. On the other hand, alcohol has an export value and will not only save the country reserves but also generate them (the price of alcohol is twice that of petrol in the international market).

3.4.8 Storage Problems

The gasohol programme will require additional transport costs as compared with petrol gasolene because the amount of water in a truck load of gasohol becomes a critical factor.

In Brazil gasohol preparation is carried out in one of two ways. Some distributors have blending tanks whereby gasoline and alcohol are mixed prior to truck loading. Other distributors do not have a separate blending tank; addition of gasoline and alcohol is flow-controlled during the truck filling operation. Neat alcohol is distributed to gas stations (250 late 1980) using the facilities (storage tank and pump) previously employed by premium gasoline.

Brazilian alcohol production is running ahead of storage capacity especially in the North East, the poorest region, where petrol demand is low. The miscalculation of the IAA on storage capacity has also given rise to serious problems in other states, such as São Paulo where distillers are threatened with having to halve operations. The Government was forced to authorize the export of 500 million litres albeit at twice the price of imported oil (in 1979). In 1978 in the Pernambuco about 51 million litres of anhydric alcohol—50% of the total production—had to be stored because of lack of transport facilities to other states. These examples illustrate the difficulties caused by lack of infrastructure, although government officials now claim the programme of alcohol distillation is sufficiently flexible to adjust to the different circumstances. Recently the government has been encouraging the construction of mini-distilleries with capacities of up to $5m^3/day$ to meet local demand and to avoid, among other things, the transport problem.

Additionally, storage equivalent to 50% of the annual alcohol output is required because sugarcane cannot be stored easily for long before it begins to decay and ferment, and sugar mills and distilleries therefore work a 6-month harvest period.

3.4.9 *Alcohol Production*

The production of alcohol in Brazil has varied quite considerably throughout the years, reflecting international sugar and oil prices. In 1930/32 production was 33 million litres, 126.8 million in 1940/41, 140 million in 1950/51; 456.3 million in 1960/61; 637.2 million in 1970/71 and 555.6 million in 1975/76. Production had been increasing steadily over the years prior to the introduction of the PNA, after which production and status of alcohol was to increase and change dramatically. In 1981 4.2 X 10⁹ litres were produced.

Figure 3.3 illustrates this new alcohol situation well, showing the three distinct phases: (a) the pre-alcohol period prior to 1975, when alcohol was considered a by-product; (b) the implementation phase (1975–1979); and (c) the Pro-álcool implementation period (1979–1985) which reflects the growth of alcohol supply from the independent distillers supplied solely by new sugarcane plantations. It also can be seen from the figure that the projected cassava-alcohol production in 1985 (a new element in the alcohol production) is about 0.3 million m³.

Table 3.2 shows the main output forecasts for 1980–1985 including that of the chemical industry (note that forecast consumption for this sector varies from 1–3 X 10⁹ litres of alcohol), blending and alcohol fuelled automobile fleets (see also Table 3.1). The 10.7 X 10⁹ litres (8.4 million tons) of alcohol planned for 1985 could account for 4% of the total primary energy demand requirements in Brazil— but according to Table 3.1 it would be 2.1% only. If the target is achieved it would still make Brazil the world's largest alcohol producing country in 1985 (50% at least of the world's 16 million m³ production would come from Brazil).

The present 2.2 million ha under sugar cultivation is to be increased to 3.5 million ha (9.3% of the useful agricultural land). The potential available area for sugarcane is about 20 million ha. The production capacity in January 1980,

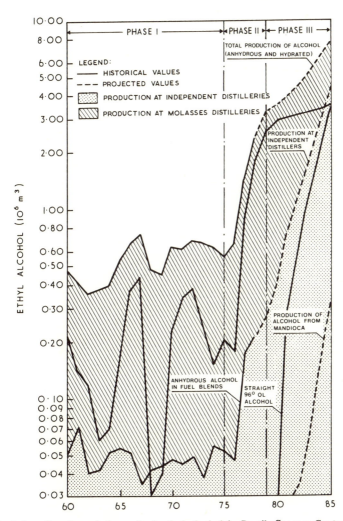

Fig. 3.3   Supply and demand of ethyl alcohol in Brazil. *Source*: Centro de Tecnologia Promon.

Table 3.2 The Proálcool programme (forecast outputs)

	1980	1981	1982	1983	1984	1985
Total ethanol product (litres $\times$ 10^9)	3.8	4.7	5.5	6.7	8.5	10.7
Chemical industry (litres $\times$ 10^9)	0.3	0.6	0.8	1.0	1.2	1.5
Anhydric ethanol (for intended 20% blending to petrol (litres $\times$ 10^9)	3.1	3.2	3.2	3.2	3.2	3.1
Volume left for 100% fuelling (litres $\times$ 10^9)	0.4	0.9	1.5	2.5	4.1	6.1
New Cars to be produced for 100% ethanol fuelling (thousand units)	207	233	253	287	346	380
Retro-fitting to be made for 100% ethanol fuelling (thousand units)	60	67	80	80	87	87
Cumulative fleet using 100% ethanol (thousand units)	267	564	891	1249	1670	2121
Required ethanol volume (litres $\times$ 10^9)	1.0	2.1	3.2	4.5	6.1	7.6
Maximum blending percentage to petrol	15.9	12.9	9.3	7.5	8.0	9.7

Source: Gooding, 1980.

including the projects accepted by Proálcool, was 5818 million litres in 247 plants (autonomous and dependent). The centre–south region accounts for 64–70% of that capacity, of which the State of São Paulo accounts for 2698 million litres (46.5% of national capacity), with ninety-eight projects implemented or being implemented.

The percentage of alcohol in the mixture with gasoline has varied from a mere 0.3% of total gasoline consumption in 1969 to 9.97% in 1978 and estimated 14.12% in 1979. The state of São Paulo due to its overcapacity has historically been the front runner in alcohol blendings. In 1967 blendings reached 13.5% (national average was 6.2%) and 10% in 1977 (4.3% national average). In all other states—particularly the north–east where car ownership is low—alcohol consumption is much lower.

3.4.10 *Perspectives (Maura Leitâo, 1979)*

By 1985 there will be a need to have two different 'fuels' for distribution: gasoline with 20% pure anhydric alcohol to be used by the automobile industry in modified or completely redesigned alcohol-powered engines, and pure hydrated alcohol to be used in the chemical sector. The production of any one of these two combustibles will depend on the total alcohol production capacity, particularly hydrated alcohol, the capacity of the automobile manufacturing industry to manufacture engines on a large scale, and the ability of governmental action in overcoming existing structural problems.

If present patterns of energy continue to grow as in recent years—it seems likely to increase at least 5% annually—some 22×10^9 litres will be needed by 1985. To have a significant effect at least 20% of the mixture must be alcohol (but according to Table 3.1 it is only 9.7%).

If the installed capacity is to reach 11.5×10^9 litres, as some estimates predict, some 5.8×10^9 litres would need to be installed up to 1982 if it is to be fully operational by 1985. That will require the installation of far more distilleries annually than has been the case so far.

By 1985 about 13 million vehicles may be on the roads (7 million in 1977) of which 4 million may be alcohol

fuelled—2.1 million on pure alcohol—an increase of almost
8 million new cars. Bearing in mind that it takes about
3 years to develop an 'alcohol engine' production on a large
scale, such work must begin quite early in the 1980s if targets
are to be met. The industry in spite of having signed a con-
tract to put 280000 alcohol-powered cars on the road in
the early 1980s does not seem totally committed. Reasons
for this included initial resistance by the customers to buying
something new, lack of infrastructure and some doubts in
the PNA ability to supply alcohol—and a perception that
the government was not committed to carry out the programme to its fullest extent, although presently the government shows signs of firmer commitment.

High investment and the marginal economics of alcohol
together with financial difficulties are further constraints to
be taken into account. Original regional development objectives are far from being met. Distilleries are being installed
where there is already a concentration such as in São Paulo,
hence contributing to further regional inequalities. Massive
public aid has gone into private ventures, and led critics to
argue that the tradition of 'privatizing profits and socializing
losses' has been the rule in this sector, alongside resistance to
any change that might lead to social redistribution of
resources. Recently in response to such criticism, the government has been paying more attention to the land-ownership
question, and encouraging the establishment of production
centres in joint ownership.

The magnitude of Proálcool will also put a severe strain on
the technical and managerial resources in both the industrial
and agricultural aspects of alcohol production and calls for
urgent training programmes to develop the skills necessary to
carry out the programme to its fullest extent.

Perhaps the greatest doubt about the whole PNA venture
concerns its ability to contribute a real reduction in the out-
flow of dollars or even to economize upon oil imports. The
substitution of petroleum fuels (its chief objectives) must be
considered in a much broader context than it has been done
so far.

References

Almeida, H. de (1979), 'O fortalecimento do Programa Nacional do Álcool', *Brasil Açúcareiro*, **94** (2), 15-22.

Almeida, H. de (1979), 'Proalcool', *Brasil Açúcareiro*, **94** (4).

Anon. (1979), 'Brazil's engineers span the world', *Brazil Journal*, **37** (364), 11-16.

Anon. (1979), 'Foreign investment. Further impetus to economy', *Brazil Journal*, **37** (365), 31-4.

Anon. (1979), 'South America, set for growth?', *Chemical Week*, 23 May, 15-29.

Anon. (1979), 'Programa Nacional do Álcool. Decreto No. 83700', *Brazil: Official Gazette*, 5 July.

Bazin, M. (1979), 'Running on alcohol', *Nature*, **282** (5739), 550-1.

Benemann, J. R. (1980), 'Proalcool, the Brazilian alcohol programme', *Biosources Digest*, **2** (3), 156-79.

Bôto Dantas, R. (1979), 'Alcool e otras fontes alternativas do energia, como substitutivas de petroleo', *Brasil Açúcareiro*, **94** (4), 32.

Bôto Dantas, R. (1980), 'Production of alcohol, the Brazilian experience', *International Sweetner Alcohol Conference: The Future of Sugar*, April, London.

Büchel, H. K. (1980), 'Agricultural products, raw material and energy source of the future', *Chemistry International*, No. 5, 17-25.

CENAL (1980), 'Proalcool, informaçôes ao empresariado', *Brasil Açúcareiro*, **95** (3), 112-31.

Coulson-Thomas, C. (1980), 'Brazilian business opportunities in the 1980s', *The Metra Consulting Group and International Joint Ventures*.

Drevon, J. J. and Thery, D. (1977), 'Ecodevelopment and industrialisation, renewability and new uses of biomass', *Ecodevelopment Study No. 9*, CIRED, Paris.

Gochnarg, I. (1979), 'The Brazilian Alcohol programme', *Biomass for Energy Conference (C-20)*, Royal Society, July, London.

Gonzaga Bertelli, L. (1980), 'A politica do alcool do Brasil', *Legenda*, **3** (23), 18-20.

Gooding, K. (1980), 'Energy review', *Financial Times*, 4 January, London.

Lindeman, R. A. and Rocchicciolo, C. (1979), 'Ethanol in Brazil, a brief summary of the state of the industry in 1977', *Biotechnology and Bioengineering*, **21**, 1107-19.

Lloyd International (1979), 'Brazil', *Bank of London and South America Review*, **13** (11).

Maura Leitâo, D. (1979), 'O etanol como fonte de energia. O programa nacional de alcool (pt. 2)', *Brasil Açúcareiro*, **93** (2).

Mont Alegre, O. (1978), 'Brazil's sugar industry', *Brazil Journal,* **36** (358).

Nicholson, B. (1979), 'The struggle to build up a Brazilian technology', *Brazilian Business,* **51** (12), 7-14.

Petrobrás (1978), *Boletin Tecnico Petrobrás,* **21** (2).

Petrobrás (1980), *Fontes Alternativas de Energia, O Álcool.*

Pimentel, L. S. (1980), 'The brazilian ethanol program', *Biotechnology and Bioengineering,* **22** (10), 1989-2012.

Redfearn, J. (1980), 'Brazilian agriculture', *Nature,* **288** (5792), 638.

Sabino Ometto, J. G. (1979), 'O Futuro do Alcool', *Brasil Açúcareiro,* **92** (2), 23-5.

Smith, D. (1979), 'Ambitious plans for alternative fuels', *Financial Times,* 16 October, 10, London.

Terdre, N. (1980), 'Rum runners', *Petroleum Review,* **34** (400), 20-1.

UNCTAD (1975), 'La función del sistema de patentes en la transferencia de tecnología', UNCTAD/OMPI TD/B/AC/11/19 Review. 1. Geneva.

Yang, V. and Trindade, S. C. (1979), 'The Brazilian Alcohol Programme', *Development Digest,* **17** (3), 12-24.

Zanca, O. (1980), 'The evolution of mechanised sugarcane harvesting in Brazil', *International Sugar Journal,* **82** (973), 7-10.

4 THE ETHANOL CHEMICAL INDUSTRY

4.1 The Ethanol Alternative

Petroleum and coal have a dual industrial function, as sources of energy and feedstocks for the chemical industry. Ethanol is a rare alternative capable of fulfilling both these functions, although there are still many problems preventing this potential being realized on a large scale. For example, though alcohol fermentation is a well-understood process it remains a wasteful one. For every ton of alcohol produced 2 tons of sugar are required, a consequence of the chemistry rather than poor process efficiency alone. Thus, the cost of the substrate is of overwhelming importance. Ethanol is, none the less, presently being commercially exploited as a dual-purpose feed, although it has not as yet been proved to be financially advantageous over present oil prices. Several other possible competitive ethanol-derived chemical products exist. Although few are commercially and economically feasible, a tremendous variety of derivatives are technically possible from an ethanol base, as can be seen from Figs. 4.1, 4.2 and 4.3. Brazil is regarded as the country most likely, in present circumstances, to make commercial use of such potential.

The general production of chemicals from biomass is carried out in four stages: cultivation; fermentation; synthesis; and product preparation. All four stages must be evaluated together and not separately as is often the case. The most obvious problems arising in this combined complex are the on-stream factor and energy interaction. Sugar beet factories, for example, usually operate for a 'campaign' of 100 days per year to meet harvesting periods and cane mills from between 120–280 days per year. The capital intensive petrochemical industry invests in plant systems designed to operate

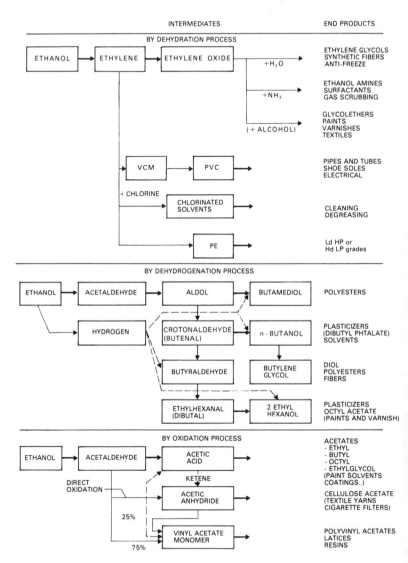

Fig. 4.1 Alcohol from biomass: production of chemicals from ethanol by major process routes. *Source*: Gira Rhone Poulenc, World Bank, 1980.

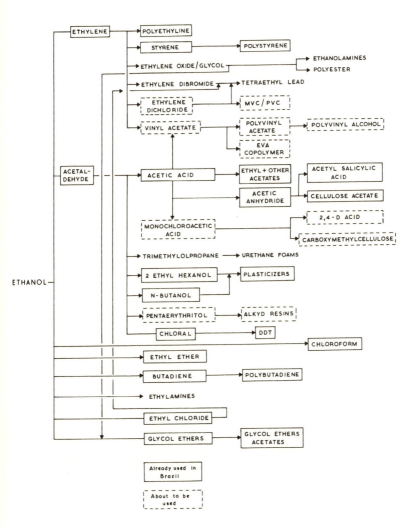

Fig. 4.2 Ethanol-based chemical routes. *Source*: Ribeiro Filho, 1979.

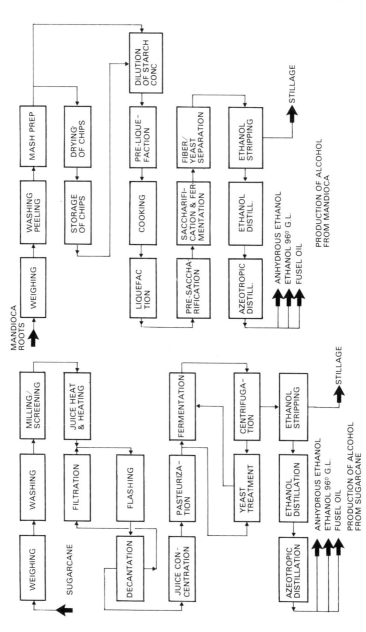

Fig. 4.3   Simplified flow diagrams of alcohol production from sugarcane and mandioca. *Source: Yang et al., 1977; Trindade, 1980b.*

for a minimum of 330 days per year and requires a continuous feedstock supply to maintain this figure. It is thus necessary to provide intermediate buffer storage or some other means of satisfying this operating requirement.

The origin of the integrated complex, therefore, will not be determined exactly by specification and capacity of product but must be considered on a case by case basis taking into account agricultural and climatic conditions, potential by-products and the comparative costs of different forms of available energy.

4.2 Origins of the Ethanol Based Chemical Industry in Brazil (Ribeiro Filho, 1979)

As mentioned previously, the ethanol industry in Brazil has been a by-product of the sugar industry and dates back to early this century where *Productos Colombina* and *Cia Química Rhodia Brasileira*, installed in the state of São Paulo, began on a small scale manufacturing perfume sprays based on ethyl chloride from ethanol.

Cia Brasileira Rhodiceta was established in 1928 and in subsequent years began to manufacture cellulose acetate using acid and acetic anhydride, both obtained from ethanol. However, the utilization of ethanol on a large industrial scale as a feedstock for the chemical industry did not begin until 1942 when *Rhodia* in São Paulo began production of alcohol from sugarcane for chemical uses. Nevertheless by 1940 the following products were being manufactured in small quantities as derivatives of ethanol: ethyl chloride, ethyl ether, acetic acid and acetic anhydride.

In the 1950s there was a great boom in the industry which, at that time, was producing a large variety of products. In 1952 *Usina Victor-Sence* of *Conceigao de Macabu* (Rio) inaugurated a plant to produce acetic acid and butyl acetate from ethanol. It was already commercially producing butanol and acetone from molasses fermentation. From the mid 1950s to late 1960s there was an expansion phase due partly to the low price of alcohol which made possible the implementation on a greater scale of new projects based on ethanol. This had a formidable effect. In 1958 *Union Carbide do Brasil* installed two alcohol ethylene units to supply its low density polyethylene plant and *Cia Brasileira de Estireno* also installed one in 1959, to supply its styrene plant. Ethylene production by means of ethanol dehydration was started in 1962 by *Industrias Químicas Electrocloko* and a vinyl acetate unit started by *Rhodia* utilized acetylene and acetic acid obtained from ethanol. In 1965 *Cia Pernambucana de Borracha Sintética (Coperbo)* started to produce butadiene from ethyl alcohol, including the production of the intermediate acetaldehyde. *Elekeiroz do Nordeste* in 1969 began production of 2-ethylhexanol by means of an entirely ethanol chemical route, obtaining butanol acetic acid and ethyl acetate as by-products.

The expansion phase was altered in the early 1970s when petrochemicals began to supply the market at low prices and raw materials became scarce and costly—a 67% price increase in 1967-1969, partly due to the favourable conditions in the international sugar market. Thus ethanol based chemical products became once more uncompetitive with those of petrochemicals at a time when large petrochemical projects were being implemented in Brazil. Some units utilizing ethanol as their raw material were forced to close down—the ethylene plants of *Cia Brasileira de Estileno* in 1970; *Union Carbide* in 1971, among others. A strong comeback began in the mid 1970s with the three-fold oil price increases and consequent petroleum chemical prices, this together with the energy crisis and the non-existence of competitive ethanol-chemical processes in the international market, has led Brazilian companies and institutions to revive R&D studies in this field and again recognize the potential of ethanol as chemical feedstock.

4.3 Chemical Production (Souza Antunes, 1979; *Chemical Engineering News*, 1979)

The Brazilian programme for the chemical industry as a whole is very ambitious. For example, chemical production under the Second Plan (1974-79) was planned to show an increase of 244% for sulphuric acid, a 179% increase for chloride—from 0.212 million tons to 0.59 million tons;

for ethylene a 109% increase from 0.34 million tons to 0.7 million tons. In the mid-1970s Brazil's chemical and petrochemical industry output represented one-fifth of the total industrial production and was growing at 16% per annum as opposed to the 10% growth rate in other industrial sectors.

In 1977 Brazil's total oil refining chemical and petrochemical output was estimated at nearly 14×10^9—c. 10% of its GDP—and from 1977 to 1982 production is predicted to expand at an average of 11.5% annually, reaching some 25×10^9 in 1982. Since the late 1970s Brazil's annual investment in petrochemicals has been almost 1×10^9. The long-term development of the Brazilian petrochemical industries is focussed on the petrochemical centres established in strategic geographical areas of the country.

1 The first of such centres was erected in the city of Cubatâo (state of São Paulo) and began operation in the late 1960s.

2 The second centre located near the city of Camacari in the state of Bahia began operating in 1978. The Camacari Project will eventually double Brazil's capacity with a total investment of 3.2×10^9 including $200 million of foreign investment. It is expected that the project will earn some $80–100 million per year in export plus an additional $600 million in import savings. The total amount of savings expected from the ethanol-based sector is about $200 million in 1980–1985. Additionally the Camacari complex has been injected with more money for further expansion. In 1980 Dow Chemical was granted $170 million to expand capacity of chloride production from 0.133 million tons to 0.3 million tons per year; 'caustic' production from 0.150 to 0.333 million tons per year to start production in mid 1982; propylene oxide capacity from 0.09 million to 0.234 million tons per year to start in mid-1981, plus 0.18 million tons per year of vinyl chloride for operation in 1982; and are possibly going to build a new plant for producing ethylene from ethanol with capacity for 0.1 million tons per year.

3 The third centre is being constructed in the state of Rio Grande do Sul and would be fully operational by 1983 with a total investment of 1.5×10^9.

4.4 Ethanol Chemical Production

The agrochemical sector is relatively small compared with that of petrochemicals, and as the previous section has shown, with a flourishing and expanding petrochemical sector the agrochemical industry will be hard pressed, even with subsidies, to compete with this modern sector, at least in the short term.

Nevertheless Brazil is currently manufacturing a variety of chemicals from ethanol. It includes 146000 tons per year capacity of ethylene; 94500 tons per year of acetaldehyde; 6750 tons per year butanol; 33000 tons per year butadiene; 1880 tons per year of ethyl ethers; 3200 tons per year of glycol ethers and 60 tons per year of ethyl chloride. Table 4.1 shows in more detail the ethanol-based chemical capacity and its major uses, and Table 4.2 lists ethanol-based chemical units being installed in the period 1981–1985.

The utilization of ethanol as a chemical feedstock has not been significantly important up to 1980. The period 1971–1977 is shown in Table 4.3. Of the 637 million litres of alcohol production, 23.7% went to the chemical sector in 1971, of the 796 million litres in 1977, 20.17%—with an average of 14.9% 1971–1977. The share of the pharmaceutical sector has been much higher. It should be noted that ethanol is used in an enormous variety of industrial applications ranging from cleansing, laboratory use, to solvents etc. About 17 million litres of ethanol were consumed in 1978 in this kind of use.

By 1981 ethanol feedstock consumption is expected to triple. Government subsidies fixing the cost at 35% of that of ethylene have already resulted in large consumption increases. The substitution of ethanol for naphtha, for example, will increase about 300% by 1982. The PNA foresees 1.5×10^9 litres of alcohol being consumed by the chemical sector (estimates vary from 1 to 3×10^9 litres). But, on the whole, production will still be low compared with that of petrochemicals.

The shortcomings in oil supplies are forcing more attention to be paid to ethanol, and as new technology is developed more and more ethanol chemical products ought to become an alternative to petrochemicals, particularly in the Second and Third World. As pretroleum prices rise, and once the present planned petrochemical plants are built, it is likely that more investment will be channelled to this sector. For example, *Petrobrás* is intensively involved in and has developed an entirely new ethylene from ethanol process, which is within the reach of companies who might be interested to use it in Brazil. It would have a capacity of 60000 tons/year. A *Petrobrás* subsidiary, *Salgema Industrias Químicas SA* in Maceió (Alagoas) is building a plant for the production of dichlorethane which will be comparable to equivalent foreign plants in terms of production capacity and operation costs, but its total cost is 3.5 times less.

In spite of many obstacles, therefore, the potential of ethanol as a basic feedstock for the chemical industry in Brazil is significant and as oil reserves dwindle will be of increasing importance.

4.5 Chemical Prices (*European Chemical News,* 1979)

There are two major obstacles to ethanol becoming a major or principal chemical feedstock, its price and the present state of technology. At the moment the costs of ethanol production are often greater than its final value, especially in the case of ethanol obtained directly from sugarcane. The economic question is complicated by the fact that whilst chemically ethanol is a single compound, economically it is two. First there is the alcohol obtained as a by-product of sugar production and secondly the alcohol obtained as a primary direct product from sugarcane. The former, whose price is linked to that of sugar, is usually cheaper.

Costs, at least in the short term, will continue to be a major obstacle, therefore subsidies must continue if alcohol is to continue to play its politically strategic role for Brazil. The question arises as to the level of such subsidies. To this end *Petrobrás* has carried out technical and economic evaluations in a number of ethanol based reactions with the aim of deciding which products can already compete with petroleum derived ones or which could become competitive in the future. These studies were also intended to evaluate the

Table 4.1 Ethanol-based chemical industry in Brazil

Product	Plant				Remarks
	Company	Capacity ton/yr	Process	Uses	
Ethylene	Union Carbide do Brasil SA	23 000	U.C.C.	IDPE	The unit operated from 1958 to 1969
	Indústrias Químicas Eletro Cloro SA	10 000	Scientific design	MDPE	In operation since 1962
	Companhia Brasileira de Estireno SA	4000	Koppers	Ethylbenzene-styrene	The unit operated from 1959 to 1970. The operation was taken over in 1978
	Salgema Indústrias Químicas SA	60 000	Petrobrás Cenpes	Ethylene dichloride	Scheduled start-up: 1981
	Companhia Pernambucana de Borracha Síntética-Coperbo	30 000	Coperbo	Vinyl acetate	Adaptation of butadiene facilities, already existent; scheduled start-up: 1982
Acetaldehyde	Rhodia Indústrias Químicas e Texteis SA	40 000	Rhone Poulenc	Acetic acid and solvents	In operation
	Hoechst do Brasil Químicas e Farmac. SA	4200	Hoechst	Acetic acid and solvents	In operation
	Usina Victor Sence SA	360	Melle	Acetic acid and solvents	In operation
	Companhia Pernambucana de Borracha Síntética-Coperbo	50 000	UCC	Acetic acid-vinyl acetate	The unit operated from 1965 to 1971. Being reactivated at present

Product	Company	Capacity	Licensor	Use	Observations
Octanol (2-ethylhexanol)	Elekeiroz do ne Ind. Química SA	3300	Melle	Plasticizers	In operation. Expansion to 16500 ton/yr at present
Butanol	Elekeiroz do ne Ind. Química SA	150	Melle	Solvents and plasticizers	By-product of Octanol Unit. Expansion to 730 ton/yr
	Rhodia Indústrias Químicas e Texteis SA	4800	Melle	Solvents	In operation
	Hoechst do Brasil Química e Farmac. SA	1530	Hoechst	Solvents	In operation
Butadiene	Companhia Pernambucana de Borracha Sintética-Coperbo	33000	UCC	Polibutadiene	The unit operated from 1963 to 1971. There is a project to adapt it in order to produce ethylene (see above)
Ethyl ether	Rhodia Indústrias Químicas e Texteis SA	1400	Rhone Poulenc	Chemicals and pharmaceuticals	In operation. There is a project for expansion and modernization of the unit
	Imbel-Ind. de Material Bélico do Exército	480		Explosives	In operation
Ethylene glycol monoethylether	Oxiteno SA. Indústria e Comercio	1300	Halcon	Acetates and solvents	In operation since 1973
Diethyleneglycol monoethylether	Oxiteno SA Indústria e Comércio	1900	Halcon	Acetates and solvents	In operation since 1973
Ethyl chloride	Companhia Brasileira de Estireno SA	60	CBE	Catalyst in ethylbenzene production	In operation (pilot plant)

Source: Ribeiro Filho, 1979.

Table 4.2 Ethanol-based chemical units being installed in Brazil, 1981–1985

Company	Onstream	Product	Capacity t/a	Total ethanol consumption	Process
Union Carbide	Onstream	Ethylene	40000	90000	Union Carbide
Salgema	September 1981	Ethylene	60000	136200	Petrobrás
Elekeiroz NE	1982	Octanol	13200	39000	Rhone-Poulenc
Elekeiroz NE	1982	Butanol	580		
		Ethyl acetate	1320		
		Acetic acid	440		
Cloteril	1982	Acetaldehyde	10200	15700	Cloteril
		Acetic acid	13300		
		Ethyl/butyl acetate	8200		
Oxiteno	1983	Acetaldehyde	46000	67600	Oxiteno
		Butanol	25000		
		Acetic acid	14000		
Coperbo	1984	Acetaldehyde	48000	134700	Coperbo
		Ethylene	32000		
		Acetic acid	60000		
		Ethyl acetate	1350		
		Butanol	220		
BASF	1984	Ethylamines	8262	4770	BASF
Química da Bahia	1984	Ethylamines	7260	3077	

Source: Chemical Engineering, 1981.

Table 4.3 Production and consumption of ethanol in the industrial sector, 1971–1977 (thousand litres)

Year	National production	Chemical industry					Pharmaceutical industry and others			
		Polyethylene	Organic solvents	Buthyl rubber[1]	Percentage used by chemical industry	Total for chemical industry	Total	%	Grand total (6 + 7)	Total % (5 + 8)
	(1)	(2)	(3)	(4)	(5)	(6)	(7)	(8)	(9)	(10)
1971	637200	61000	48100	41900	23.70	151000	170000	26.68	321000	50.38
1972	613100	45500	49500	38000	21.69	133000	182000	29.69	315000	51.38
1973	681000	–	45500	–	6.68	45500	195000	28.63	240000	35.30
1974	666000	–	48000	–	7.21	48000	332000	49.85	380000[2]	57.05
1975	625000	5000	49500	1500	8.96	56000	329000	52.64	385000[2]	61.60
1976	555600	21600	63400	2275	15.71	87275	366725	66.01	454000[2]	81.70
1977	796000	89800	68300	2450	20.17	160550	389450	48.53	550000[3]	69.09
Totals	4573900	283900	372300	86125	14.90	681325	1964175	42.94	2645500	57.84

Notes: [1] Ethyl ether and others.
[2] Adjusted figures.
[3] Estimated figures.
[4] Estimated figures.

Source: Column 1, 5, 8. Associación Brasileira da Industria Quimica e Productos Derivados & Empresas 1978 (1979) Table 3.11, p. 3.21. Column 2, 3, 4, 6, 7, 9. Ibid. Table 3.10, p. 3.20.

effect of the ethanol subsidy applicable in Brazil. For each process considered calculations were done with ethanol prices of \$293/ton and \$170/ton, being the existing prices in September 1978, without and with the subsidy respectively.

Their study showed that ethanol routes for acetaldehyde and acetic acid products were competitive with petrochemical routes. But butanol, ethylene and butadiene production from ethanol would require an alcohol subsidy to be economically viable.

4.6 Process Technology (*European Chemical News*, **1979**; *Chemical Engineering*, **1980**)

The state of technology represents the second great obstacle in the way of ethanol becoming a more important feedstock. Fortunately technical improvements are possible at all stages in the preparation and utilization of ethanol—from the growing of the sugarcane through to the distillation of the ethanol. Below we list some of the new technical developments which are in the pipeline and which might significantly improve ethanol's economic competitiveness.

The level of sugarcane productivity varies quite significantly. If average yields could be improved 100% ethanol costs would improve 26%. An increase in the sucrose content from 130 kg/tonne to 160 kg/tonne—which is widely considered feasible—would improve ethanol production costs a further 10%.

Fermentation processes for the production of ethanol have developed considerably in recent years, although basic characteristics will be likely to remain the same. Up to now raw cane sugar appears to be the only viable feedstock for ethanol fermentation, but new developments are continuously taking place. Preparation of the feedstock normally requires the extraction of the sugar, but new ideas suggest that only partial breakdown of the cane is necessary before extraction and fermentation can be brought about simultaneously by the EX-FERM technique (Rolz and de Cabrera, 1980). This technique is energy saving compared with the normal process of sugar manufacture. After preparation of feedstock, which varies according to the type of the raw material, Saccharomyces yeast strains are used to ferment the carbohydrate. Considerable improvement in the fermentation is possible with the selection of more efficient alcohol-tolerant yeast strains, but even certain bacteria such as *Zymomonas mobilis* (Lee *et al.*, 1977; Rogers *et al.*, 1979) and *Clostridium thermocellum* (Zeikus, 1980) can be employed with improved productivity. Once the ethanol concentration in a reactor reaches 15% by weight the fermentation will stop. Until recently, most alcoholic fermentations were carried out in the batch mode but significant developments have been made for semi-continuous and continuous operation.

In a conventional batch fermentation process the concentration of alcohol in the final mixture was only about 7–8% requiring a three stage distillation to produce pure alcohol. Recently Tate and Lyle have developed a continuous fermentation process for ethanol and they believe that such a continuous process can produce 12% alcohol in a plant one-tenth of the size of conventional units and with a productivity 2.5 times as high, with lower capital investment, less distillation and smaller volume of effluent.

Humphreys and Glasgow Ltd have also designed a 50000 ton/year alcohol plant based on carbohydrate feedstocks which can be utilized to produce ethanol competitively, it seems, with petroleum derived products. The study is based on commercially proven processes, mainly from Brazil. The fermentation technology came from the Brazilian company *Deon Houlett*. Humphreys and Glasgow Ltd think it is feasible with present oil prices.

Likewise Japan Gas Corporation (JGC) has developed a 'successful and economically feasible' process for the production of ethylene from fermentation ethanol. The process has been tested as a pilot plant in Brazil, in co-operation with the *Instituto de Pesquisas Tecnologicas* (São Paulo) using industrial grade ethanol produced locally.

Stone and Webster Engineering have developed a new process for the production of fuel-grade ethanol from grain, resulting in energy savings up to 25%. Major advantages are the integration of the energy-intensive drying, evaporation and distillation steps. Both marketable and damaged grain can be used as feedstock for the process, which results in a dry distillers grain by-product for use as a high protein feed for cattle. It is possible also, at minimal cost, to recover carbon dioxide from the process.

Padua University researchers have also been very successful in developing new processes. They have developed a method that will use cornmeal to reduce the energy requirement from 4.5–11MJ/litre to 3.4MJ/litre. A gaseous ethanol is passed through a bed of cornmeal containing 10–20% water, which can be regenerated by hot air with an energy expenditure of 0.53MJ/litre product. Another improvement is the Canadian 'Tilby' method which is a process that allows processing to take part in one stage instead of the normal three, with 40% reduced energy cost.

The Scientific Design Co. (New York) has also come out with a new catalyst—offering increased productivity and operational life—and a new reactor design which cuts the cost of ethylene produced by the dehydration of ethanol. In contrast to the old catalyst the new one has a greater activity and in the region of optimal operation its mixtures are more productive. The ethanol selectivity of by-products has been reduced from about 6% to 3% resulting in significant savings in capital utilized and quantity of waste produced.

Recently the W. S. Atkins Group have developed the ATPAL (Atkins Power Alcohol) low-energy system for ethanol production from biomass. They claim to be able to produce ethanol using lower energy consumption than conventional routes, up to 75% less in some circumstances.

Hoechst AG and its engineering subsidiary UHDE GmbH have reported their process which reduces by a third the energy needed for distillation. This system requires 0.9 kg of steam per kg of ethanol as compared to the conventional requirement of 3.5 kg of steam per kg of ethanol. Table 4.4 shows the range of achievements of various alternative distillation systems.

A joint company formed between Allied Breweries and Contractors John Brown, Allcon Ltd have also built a fully continuous pilot plant which is under test in the Philippines.

Table 4.4   Energy efficiency of alternative distillation systems

System	Energy consumption tonne steam (Sat.40 Psig) per m^3 ethanol 100%	Technical availability
Atmospheric distillation, cellulose dehydration	1.0	Laboratory stage
Atmospheric distillation, CaO dehydration	1.3	Laboratory stage
Differential pressure fermentation, vacuum distillation	1.6	Laboratory stage
Differential pressure fermentation, atmospheric distillation	3.6	Laboratory/ pilot
Vacuum fermentation, atmospheric distillation	3.7	Laboratory/ pilot
Reboiler, feed preheating and optimization	3.5	Commercial
Live steam distillation	4.5–5.0	Commercial

Source: Trindade, *et al.*, 1980.

4.7 Areas of Potential Technical Improvement

Such recent developments are very encouraging for the ethanol-based industry as a whole, particularly for the chemical sector, so far as cost and energy balance is concerned.

Ethanol is produced in Brazil using traditional process technology and the industry is most conservative in its attitude towards changes. Part of the problem is that there is limited trained manpower to handle an improved process. Little instrumentation is used and steam is produced in low-pressure boilers, with no treated water, which are equipped with primitive types of furnaces, burning bagasse with 50% moisture content and often requiring wood logs and fuel oil as a complement for starting up. Fermentation equipment is invariably made in mild steel and are open vessels with a consequent limited life and poor operational characteristics. Currently operated distillation units possess steam requirements of the order of 5.0 ton steam/m^3 ethanol produced. The application of relatively simple measures such as feed preheating, reboiler use etc. could cut vapour requirements by about 30% (see Table 4.4).

Traditional fermentation processes in Brazil could be greatly improved, with continuous fermentation, vacuum fermentation and the use of yeasts resistant to higher alcohol concentration. Figure 4.3 shows two simplified diagrams of alcohol production from sugarcane and cassava in Brazil. Both processes encompass four steps: preparation; juice conditioning; fermentation and distillation (sugarcane); preparation, conversion, fermentation and distillation (cassava) and it is clear from Fig. 4.4 where the improvements could be made.

The main reasons for the currently experienced low industrial productivity and hence large capital costs in the production of ethanol are:

— failure to achieve sufficiently high cell densities during fermentation;
— relatively low ethanol tolerance and low maximum substrate uptake rates of the microorganisms involved;

Therefore greater effort should be made to:

— increase cell densities in the fermentation;
— reduce product inhibition;
— identify alternative microbiological systems with higher substrate uptake rates and higher ethanol resistances.

Other fermentation improvements under study include semipermeable membranes and molecular sieves.

4.8 Main Ethanol-chemical Processes Used in Brazil (Ribeiro Filho, 1979)

On the production of chemical products efforts are being channelled to production of acetaldehyde, ethylene, acetic acid, vinyl acetate, 2-ethyl hexanol, dichloroethane PVC, butanol etc. (see Table 4.1). Some details of specific processes are given below.

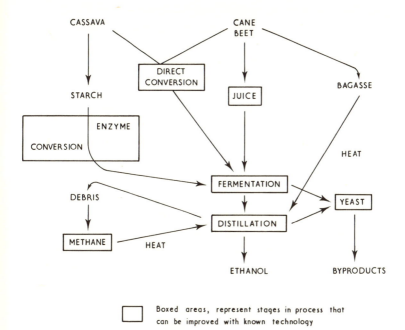

Fig. 4.4   Areas of potential technical improvement.

4.8.1 *Ethylene production*

The Electro Cloro's traditional ethylene production is by direct dehydration of ethanol using a silica-alumina catalyst:

$$C_2H_5OH \rightarrow C_2H_4 + H_2O - 45.64 \text{ kJ/mol}$$

The reaction is carried out at temperatures between 300–360°C and low pressure over a catalyst bed in a tubular reactor. It results in the formation of several by-products such as coke, ethyl ether, carbon monoxide and carbon dioxide.

Ethylene is produced 97-98% pure, further distillation being necessary to give about 99% pure product. Petrobrás Research Centre (Cenpes) has developed an adiabatic variation of this process, spurred on by the high costs of the earlier isothermic process. *Salgema Industrias Químicas* (an affiliate of *Petrobrás Química*) has set up a $27 million plant to produce ethylene from ethanol at Maccio in north-east Brazil. It will go into production in late 1981, and have a capacity of 60000 tons per year from 110000 tons per year of ethanol, using the adiabatic dehydration process.

4.8.2 *Acetaldehyde*

The production process used in Brazil comprises the catalytic dehydrogenation of ethanol in the steam phase, according to the following reaction:

$$CH_3-CH_2OH \xrightarrow[\substack{CuCr \\ catalyst}]{260°C} CH_3-CHO + H_2$$
$$\text{ethanol} \qquad\qquad \text{acetaldehyde}$$

Efficiency for acetaldehyde is 85–92% for liquid by-products 12–6% and gaseous by-products 3–2%. The main by-products are ethylacetate and acetic acid, and in smaller quantities, butyraldehyde, methylethylketone, ketone, butanol, methane, ethylene, carbon dioxide and carbon monoxide.

4.8.3 *Acetic Acid*

The process developed by *Petroquisa* consists of an improvement of the existing domestic acetic acid technique based on the liquid phase oxidation of acetaldehyde.

A basic feature of this process is the utilization of the oxidation gas (air), prior to the reaction, to recover the acetaldehyde contents of the reactor effluent. The unit operates at low pressure and temperature and a special design of the sparged reactor allows it to operate with high gas velocity without excessive acetaldehyde entrainment.

A new catalyst system is being developed for obtaining a selective improvement. The liquid effluent from the reactor contains mainly acetic acid and small amount of by-products, such as formic acid, methyl acetate and others.

4.8.4 *Butanol and Octanol*

Production is obtained through traditional processes. Acetaldehyde—by dehydrogenation of ethanol—and crotonaldehyde

—by aldolization of crotonaldehyde as subsequent dehydrogenation of alcohol—are initially produced. And then hydrogenations of crotonaldehyde whereby the *n*-butanol and butyraldehyde are obtained, the latter by complete dehydrogenation. If the purpose is primarily production of *n*-butanol, butyraldehyde may be recycled until complete extinction. But if it is intended to obtain octanol (2-ethylhexanol) hydrogenation is controlled in such a way as to maximize butyraldehyde production which, however, does not prevent formation of *n*-butanol as a by-product.

4.8.5 *Butadiene*

In this process utilized by Coperbo, the following chemical reaction occurs:

$$CH_3CHO + CH_3CH_2OH \rightarrow CH_2CHCH=CH_2 + H_2O$$
acetaldehyde   ethanol   butadiene   water

Such reaction seems to take place in two phases:

(i) $2CH_3CHO \rightarrow CH_3CHCH=CHCHO + H_2O$
acetaldehyde   crotonaldehyde   water

(ii) $CH_3CH=CHCHO + CH_3CH_2OH \rightarrow$
crotonaldehyde   ethanol

$$CH_2=CHCH=CH_2 + CH_3CHO + H_2O$$
butadiene   acetaldehyde   water

The final stage of the process comprises dehydration of ethanol to acetaldehyde. The second stage involves manufacture of butadiene proper. Total efficiency of ethanol based butadiene is between 50–63%, including loss in efficiency in acetaldehyde production and losses relating to product recuperation and transfer.

4.9 Methanol

There is much discussion in Brazil nowadays about a large project for producing methanol by pyrolysis of wood from fast-growing eucalyptus trees. The Brazilian Energy Supplying Company (CESP) has drawn up a plan according to which sixty-five methanol plants could be erected by 1985, an investment of 15×10^9, with capacity to produce 45.5 million tons of methanol per year which, probably, could replace some third of Brazil's oil requirements by 1985. To reach this goal, an estimated 5.5 million ha (0.64% of Brazil's area) will need to be cultivated with eucalyptus trees. Twenty tons of eucalyptus trees could produce 8.3 tons of methanol. A first 2000 tons/day methanol plant is already being built.

4.10 Conclusions

Seen within its historical context the development of Brazil's sucrochemical industry reflects more than any other technology her specific socio-economic environment, certainly more than does the petrochemical technology and industry —mostly of foreign origin. If Brazil is to fully realize the national potential in its sucrochemical industry, and make it competitive with petrochemicals, even greater technical efforts and developments are required. If this does occur then Brazil will truly become the world leader in this kind of technology.

References

Anderson, E. (1979), 'Brazil sets lofty goals for ethanol', *Chemical Engineering News,* **57** (32), 15–16.

Arnold, M. (1980), 'Natural products, plenty more where that came from', *European Chemical News* (Technology Supplement), 22 December, 55–6, **58**.

Associación Brasileira da Industria Quimica e Productos Derivados & Empressas (1979). *A Industria Quimica Brasileira.*

Bôto Dantas, R. (1980), 'Production of alcohol, the Brazilian experience', *International Sweetner, Alcohol Conference. The Future of Sugar,* April, London.

Centro de Tecnologia (PRONON) (1979), 'Alcohol, the Brazilian way out of the energy crisis', *UNITAR Conference on Longterm Resources, Montreal (Canada),* 26-27 December.

Chemical Engineering (1979), 'South American broadens petrochemical scope', 25 March, 120-2, 288.

Ibid. (1980), 'Brazil expanding use of alcohol as chemical feedstock', 2 June, 30c.

Ibid. (1980), 'New ethanol route wears low energy label', 17 November, 103.

Ibid. (1981), 'Energy required, ethanol biomass', 9 February, 17.

European Chemical News (1979), 'Humphreys and Glasgow ready with fermentation design', 3 December, 21.

Ibid. (1979), 'Tate and Lyle develops continuous fermentation ethanol process', 11 June, 21.

Ibid. (Petrochemical Supplement) (1979), 'Ethanol Chemistry to be or not be be?', 17 December, 36, 40-1.

Ibid. (1980), 'Low cost ethanol process from Stone and Webster', 8 September, 30.

Ibid. (1980), 'World biotechnology markets to blossom in the next decade', 15 September, 15.

Ibid. (1980), 'JGC offers economic process for ethylene from ethanol', 29 September, 30.

Ibid. (1980), 'Ethanol from wheat costs three times higher than gasoline', 10 November, 35.

Ibid. (1980), 'Cane sugar the only viable feedstock for ethanol fermentation', 17 November, 38.

Ibid. (1980), 'Cornmeal absorbent cuts ethanol energy demand', 24 November, 24.

Humphreys and Glasgow Ltd (1980), 'Agrosources Chemical', Personal Communication.

Lee, K. J. *et al.* (1979), 'Ethanol production by *Zymomonas mobilis* in continuous culture at high glucose concentrations', *Biotechnology Letters,* 1, 421.

Kockar, N. K. (1980), 'Ethylene from ethanol, the economics are improved', *Chemical Engineering,* 87 (2), 28 January, 80-1.

Parker, K. J. (1980), 'Probable future of natural products and chemical raw materials', *13th TNO Conference,* Rotterdam, 27-28 March.

Paulinyi, E. T. and Paulinyi, E. (1977), 'Alternativa para a petroquimica: a sucroquimica como resposta tecnologica apropianda ao Brasil', *Brasil Açúcareiro,* May, 41-6.

Ribeiro Filho, F. A. (1979), 'The ethanol-based chemical industry in Brazil', *UNIDO Workshop on Fermentation Alcohol, 26-30 March,* DOC.ID/WG 293/4, Vienna.

Rogers, P. L. *et al.* (1979), 'Kinetics of alcohol production by *Zymomonas mobilis* at high sugar concentrations', *Biotechnology Letters,* **1**, 165.

Rolz, C. and Cabrera, S. (1980), 'Ethanol from sugarcane: flask experiments using the EX-FERM technique', *Applied and Environmental Microbiology,* **40** (3), 466–71.

Souza Antunes, A. M. (1979), 'Alcool—alternativa para a industria quimica', *Revista de Finanças Públicas,* **39** (340), 45.

Spear, M. (1981), 'Low energy route to ethanol from biomass fermentation', *Process Engineering,* February, 85–7.

Trindade, S. *et al.* (1980a), 'Outlook of ethanol fermentation concentration technologies', *World Bio-energy Conference, 22 April,* Atlanta, Georgia.

Trinidade, S. *et al.* (1980b), 'The Brazilian alcohol program', *11th World Energy Conference,* 8–12 September, Munich.

Unger, T. (1979), 'Alcool como materia prima para industria quimica', *Brasil Açúcareiro,* 94 (1, 17–21).

Yang, V. *et al.* (1977), 'Cassava fuel alcohol in Brazil', in: *Intersociety Energy Conversion Engineering Conference—IECEC,* **12**, Washington, DC, 1977, *Proceedings,* La Grange Park, Ill., 44–53.

Zeikus, J. G. (1980), 'Chemical and fuel production by anaerobic bacteria', *Annual Review of Microbiology,* **34**, 423.

5 ETHANOL AS FUEL

5.1 Historical Background (Maura Leitâo, 1979)

Consideration of the use of ethanol as an automotive fuel is as old as the invention of the combustion engine itself. Nikolas A. Otto used pure alcohol in 1897 in his first engine. In 1907, the US Department of Agriculture published a report called the 'Use of Alcohol and Gasoline in Farm Engines', and in Britain, Ross and Ormandy in 1926 discussed the utilization of alcohol in the internal combustion engine. Bridgeman in 1936 published a paper on the 'Utilization of Ethanol Gasoline Blends' and in 1937, Alexander Ogston wrote a fascinating paper on alcohol gasoline blends. By the beginning of the World War II, the European consumption of alcohol-based fuel topped half a million tons annually.

In Brazil in 1902 a document was published on the Industrial Applications based on ethanol during a conference held in Bahia on the Sugar Industry. In 1919, in Pernambuco for the first time, the use of alcohol in official vehicles was made compulsory. During the 1920s experiments with blends (alcohol-gasoline) were taking place, albeit it only consisted of a few experimental vehicles. The first sign of ethanol utilization as an automotive fuel was in 1923 using a blend of 65% ethanol. In 1925, Ford automobile made a circuit (Rio de Janeiro–São Paulo and back) on pure alcohol. In 1930 a locomotive travelled from Rio to São Paulo utilizing methanol with a mixture of 5% ethyl ether. By the end of the 1920s, new products were being utilized such as USGA—75% alcohol and 25% ethyl ether; ROSADA, MOTOGAS, NACIONALINA, AZULINA, and MOTORINA. The precedent has been clearly set for the present situation and the future.

5.2 Technical Data (Bernhardt, 1980a, b)

Alcohol as motor fuel is a controversial issue. Considerable heated and partisan discussions are still taking place about the usefulness of alcohol as motor fuel. The 'anti-alcohol' school bring out unfavourable features such as phase separation, necessity for blending agents, starting troubles, vapour lock tendency, overheating and increased cylinder wear. The 'pro-alcohol' school generally stress the high octane rating, safety in storage and good thermal efficiency.

The balance and economics of the production and utilization of ethanol as a fuel are enhanced by its octane-boosting, temperature and fuel/air ratio properties. Because conversion efficiencies for alcohol production are too low (18% for cassava, 31% for sugarcane, for example), it is viewed by some sectors with concern, who feel that sources other than biomass should be investigated.

Tables 5.1 and 5.2 show some properties of alcohol compared with premium gasoline and properties of hydrated ethanol and regular gasoline in Brazil.

Table 5.1   Properties of alcohols compared with a premium gasoline

	MeOH	*EtOH*	*Premium gasoline*
Octane rating (unleaded)			
Research (*R*)	112	110	96
Motor (*M*)	92	90	84
(*R* + *M*)/2	102	100	90
Heat of evaporation (kJ/kg)	1109	902	864
Flame temp at 1 Bar (°C)	470	392	478
Max flame speed (m/s)	0.48	0.40	0.33
Oxygen content (wt %)	49.9	34.7	0
Fuel/air, stoichiometric	0.155	0.111	0.069

Source: Kampen, 1980.
MeOH = Methanol; EtOH = Ethanol.

Table 5.2 Properties of hydrated ethanol and regular gasoline in Brazil

		Ethanol	Regular gasoline
Water content	wt %	~6	—
Density at 15°C	g/cm³	0.8	0.735
Boiling temperature	°C	78	32–185
Heating value	Lower kJ/kg	~25 140	~42 430
Latent heat of vaporization	kJ/kg	903	376–502
Stoichiometric A/F	kg air / kg fuel	8.45	14.8
Motor octane number	MON	94	73
Research octane number	RON	111	85

Source: Volkswagen do Brasil, 1980.

5.2.1 *Engine Modification*

When blended with petrol in proportions of up to 25% (by volume) of alcohol, the advantages of greater volumetric efficiency and octane number improvement offset the lower calorific value of alcohol (26.6 MJ/kg versus petrol 44.0 MJ/kg).

With appropriate engines pure alcohol delivers 18% more power per litre than gasoline, but it is consumed at a rate which is 15–20% higher. This means that the two factors effectively cancel, leaving neither fuel with a clear advantage from an energy point of view. Above 25% the engine's power and fuel consumption begin to be affected. Nevertheless higher percentages of alcohol in motor fuel are feasible via a lean limit control system. The system requires some electronic sensing and enlarged carburettor jets, but its rapid response permits a return to low alcohol fuel with minimal fuel economy penalty.

To operate on pure alcohol, petrol engines would have to be modified at a cost between $200–400 and probably higher.

5.2.2 *Octane Number*

Due to its high octane number, alcohol is suitable for high-compression spark-ignition engines. Best advantage of this particular quality is obtained with pure alcohol in high-compression-ratio engines. The low volatability and higher flash point gives increased safety and may improve fuel economy. The lower engine temperature obtained with alcohol, because it has a higher latent heat of vapourization, results in lowered emissions of nitric oxides, less carbon deposit and lowered carbon monoxide content in the exhaust. But its high latent heat vaporization means that it has to be supplied with much higher amounts of heat to vaporize it.

5.2.3 *Power Output*

The higher latent heat of alcohols enables a significantly greater quantity of fuel to be burnt in an engine giving greater power output than gasoline. But this high latent heat can cause poor warm-up and driveability unless the carburettor and inlet systems design is modified to allow for it.

Because its heating value (hydrated alcohol) is substantially less than that of gasoline, when buying 1 litre of alcohol one obtains two-thirds of the energy of 1 litre of gasoline. Thus, by weight, one should in theory supply 69% more ethanol to the engine. In terms of volume this would be about 53% higher consumption. But due to higher compression ratio, better ignition and higher burning rate, it results in greater utilization of the energy available. This means that the ethanol engine functions more efficiently and the effective volumetric consumption is only 15–25% higher. Obviously this depends on the driving conditions and on the type of car used (for example, in Brazil, this means the Volkswagen).

5.2.4 *Stoichiometric Air/fuel Ratio*

This is the quantity of air that a fuel theoretically needs for its complete combustion. For alcohols it is richer than for gasoline. Carburettors have to be designed or adjusted accordingly. An amount of mixture weighing 1000 g prepared to give complete combustion would consist of:

937 g of air + 63 g of gasoline, or
895 g of air + 105 g of ethanol

(65% more ethanol by weight to the air taken in by the engine).

5.2.5 *Volatility*

Ethanol is a single component material with fixed boiling points (see Appendix 3), as opposed to gasoline which is a mixture and has a wide boiling range. In addition, alcohol/gasoline blends form azeotropes, causing a disproportionate increase in vapour pressure, particularly at small concentrations, thus alcohols or gasohol blends perform differently in the car. This has to be taken into account when designing fuel systems or setting fuel specifications.

5.2.6 *Miscibility*

The solubility of alcohols in gasoline is dependent on the temperature, the hydrocarbon composition of the gasoline and the water content. The presence of water particularly promotes phase separation, leading to a bottom phase containing alcohol and water to separate out from the blend. This can create serious problems in the fuel distribution system. While gasolines are completely miscible with each other—regardless of the hydrocarbon composition, their temperature or the presence of the water—contrary to alcohols, gasoline is not miscible with water.

Results in Brazil (VW) show that it is essential to preheat the mixture sufficiently so that the necessary quantity of alcohol enters the cylinder as a vapour. Without this measure it would be impossible to obtain low consumption, low emissions and good drivability.

5.2.7 *Starting Problems*

When starting an engine from cold, a certain amount of vapourized fuel needs to reach the vicinity of the spark plug, but because of ethanol's latent heat of vaporization, it cannot happen at temperatures below + 15°C, and the engine fails to start. Gasoline therefore has to be added to the intake air during starter operation. As soon as the engine fires and the starter is disconnected the supply of gasoline stops— but by that time there is sufficient heat in the combustion chamber to permit firing on the straight ethanol. The amount of gasoline needed is, however, a very small amount.

5.2.8 *Effects on Materials*

Alcohols have an adverse effect on some traditional fuel system materials, both in the cars themselves and in the fuel distribution network from refinery to service station. Thus, the gasoline resistant materials and coatings are not resistant to other fuels with different chemical compositions such as ethanol. Therefore new materials have to be examined. Volkswagen of Brazil has coated the inside of fuel tanks with a special plastic protection; the fuel lines are made of ethanol-resistant plastic; and the fuel pump and carburettor are protected by an anti-corrosive coating. In the engine itself no corrosion problems have been reported.

Another approach has been pioneered by USIMINAS who have developed a non-corrosive alcohol. The chlorides and organic acids which are responsible for the corrosive action of hydrated alcohol can be eliminated at very low cost during the distillation process. To do this, a third tower of equal size must be installed between the two conventional towers of a distillery. Alcohol passes through this third tower, the acidity being removed by an alkaline solution. After which it is purified by porcelain filters. This process will be utilized by the IAA distillery at Araras, S.P. An important advantage of producing this type of alcohol is that it would make it possible to use lower cost carbon steel in certain automobile parts, particularly carburettors, instead of the high-cost special steels, such as stainless steel and nickel alloys. (British Chamber of Commerce in Brazil, 1981.)

Ethanol on the whole is a good fuel in spite of all pitfalls and some of its properties (see Appendix 3) are even better than gasoline. Because alcohol 'boosts' the octane rating of gasoline, instead of simply selling gasoline as a higher-rate fuel, refineries can take advantage of this effect by producing a less-refined gasoline to combine with ethanol. This higher octane rating too, does not require additives such as anti-knock compounds or high-octane hydrocarbons.

5.3 The Brazilian Scene

A good deal of experience of gasohol comes from Brazil, albeit countries like the US are also actively involved. The situation in Brazil must be seen within a wider national context (Ch. 3–4). All major automobile manufacturers are heavily involved in the gasohol programme, with the undertaking to produce 250000 new engines for alcohol, plus 80000 new adaptations for 1980 alone.

The use of alcohol as fuel in Brazil has three main objectives:

1 The direct use of hydrated alcohol in motors specially designed for that purpose;
2 The participation of anhydrous alcohol in a mixture of up to 20% with gasoline;
3 To substitute a mixture of alcohol-vegetable oil for diesel oil.

The decision taken to introduce such objectives by the government was done after many positive results with alcohol engines by the Institute of Technology and the Aerospatial Technical Research Centre. Brazil's five car manufacturers co-operate fully with the government's plans, by offering models designed to run on 100% alcohol. Some nine different cars are now available in this form plus two locally made Honda motorcycles. Alcohol cars were put on sale to the general public on 1 April 1980. To start with, some incentives were given to alcohol-car buyers, the price of 1 gallon of alcohol was almost half that of gasoline—consumption as mentioned could be as high as 25% more on alcohol cars. A further encouragement was a 50% less road tax and a 36-month credit, as opposed to 12 months for petrol car buyers. There has, however, been some resistance to buying these new alcohol-fuelled cars until recently, when confidence in the fuel supply was established.

5.3.1 *The Ethanol Engines*

The Fiat 147 car was the first alcohol-powered car to be introduced in Brazil, but there are now quite a few different versions powered by alcohol—all have the 1297 cc engine.

All General Motors (Brazil) cars are designed to burn on 80% unleaded gasoline and 20% ethanol. General Motors manufacture both four- and six-cylinder engines. They believe that a compression ratio of 15:1 may not be too far away. Because the Brazilian regulations state that engines running on neat alcohol cannot be lower than 25% in fuel economy over the same engine designed to burn gasoline without higher compression ratios (that loss will be 35–40%), companies have been forced to increase efficiency.

Volkswagen of Brazil has developed its ethanol engines from two of its current gasoline engines: the water cooled Passat 1.5 litre straight four and the air cooled Beetle 1.3 litre horizontally-opposed four. For the Passat engines the compression ratio has been raised to 10.5:1 by increasing the length of the piston crown. The carburettor was recalibrated and the vapourization of the mixture is helped by the hot-air intake, but is mainly obtained by the heated walls of the intake manifold.

In the 1.3 litre horizontally-opposed air-cooled engine, the compression ratio was raised to 10:1. It uses two carburettors which result in short intake passages between the carburettors and the cylinder heads eliminating the need for heating of the intake manifold walls; the substantial heating of the intake air is enough. A temperature-controlled valve is used to change the intake air supply at full load from hot to cold, to prevent severe knocking in the engine.

5.3.2 *The Diesel Problem*

Alcohol cannot be blended with diesel fuel since its octane number will be seriously reduced, but quite recently research has been undertaken, particularly in Brazil, with very encouraging results. Consumption of diesel in Brazil at 20×10^9 litres in 1979, is higher than gasoline. It is used for light and heavy trucks, buses and other equipment and even in industry. Thus there is a strong interest to find substitutes.

Although the water content of the alcohol prevents it mixing with diesel fuel, up to 10% can be mixed if naphtha is also added to prevent the two liquids separating. Up to 40% alcohol can be used if the diesel and the alcohol systems are kept separate and the two fuels do not meet before the engine combustion chamber. This would mean either two separate injection systems or perhaps adding the alcohol to the induced air via a carburettor. However, in Sydney University Dr. Dick McCann has adapted a tractor to run on a 60/40 diesel/alcohol blending and a pick-up truck on a 94% alcohol/4% water solution. The only modifications needed to the pick-up truck were slightly enlarged carburettor jets and an increase in the compression ratio; while for the tractor some emulsifiers were needed in the fuel solution. But in Brazil it is vegetable oil which is seen as a possible solution.

5.3.3 Diesel Oil Substitutes in Brazil (Brazil Trade and Industry, 1980)

The idea is not new; in 1900 Rudolf Diesel himself ran a small engine on vegetable oil at an exhibition in Paris. Diesel engines have been investigated for a long time in Brazil by the *Instituto Nacional de Tecnologia Industrial* (INT)—of the *Secretaria de Tecnologia Industrial* (STI), which published a paper on this subject in 1942. The subject has been reactivated by STI and now several technical institutes are working in this field.

Diesel engines, which have a high compression ratio, must use fuel with a high-octane index and high calorific power, which ethanol does not have. If used as diesel substitute it would require the addition of an explosive substance in a proportion between 5–20%, the engine fuel consumption would also increase by about 60%. However, many vegetable oils have octane and calorific power values similar to those of diesel oil, which makes them, technically speaking, suitable substitutes. All of the most important vegetable oils produced in Brazil have been tested in diesel engines, with good results. Without modification they work well with blending of up to 30% vegetable oil and 70% diesel oil. With minor modifications, diesel engines can work with straight vegetable oil, albeit small problems related to carbon deposits in the combustion chamber have been reported in some cases. The most important oils under consideration are shown on Table 5.3. Dende marmeleiro (African Palm) is also important, others include 'pinhao' (*Jotropha spp.*), Copaifera, Croton and Tolouma. The aim was that by 1981 vegetable oils would meet 6% of Brazil's demand for diesel fuel increasing to 16% by 1985. It should be noted that these oils cause gum formation on the surfaces of the combustion chamber, and may need to be treated chemically in order to avoid this effect.

Other solutions under study to replace diesel oil tested by STI and other private industries include: (a) ethanol with additives (with minimal engine modification); (b) double feeding systems with two tanks—one with ethanol and the other with diesel oil; (c) partial solutions which have shown that vegetable oil can totally or partially replace diesel oil. Table 5.4 shows the diesel mixture comparisons.

5.4 Probable Future Trends (Kane, 1980)

It is quite possible that we have all the basic scientific knowledge to hand which will influence automobile fuels and lubricants between now and the next 20-30 years. Political and social factors will play a major role in the directions taken.

Currently the world transport industry is nearly totally dependent on petroleum fuels in spite of growing interest in the last few years in alternative fuels. In the next 10-15 years the first alternative form (or the transitional solution phase) of automobile fuels to appear will be pure ethanol (as in Brazil since 1980, gasohol in the US, and liquified petroleum gases (LPG) in the UK). Electricity and pure

Table 5.3 Possible substitutes for diesel oil

Cultivation	Years	Crop months	Yield tonne/ha	Calorific power kJ/kg	Calorific power kJ/lt	Specific gravity	Octane number
Cotton	1	3	0.11–0.20	34.75	31.80	0.92	44
Peanut	1	3	0.57–0.76	37.50	–	–	–
Babassu nut	7	12	0.10–0.30	35.30	32.24	0.92	45
Coconut	7	12	1.30–1.90	36.34	–	–	–
Palm	8	12	3.00–5.00	38.65	–	–	–
Sunflower	1	3	0.54–1.92	38.10	–	–	–
Castor	1	3	0.53–0.88	34.75	–	–	–
Soy-bean	1	3	0.24–0.36	36.85	33.90	0.92	35

Source: Bôto Dantas (1980).

Table 5.4 How diesel mixtures compare

Mixture	Proportion	Variation in relation to diesel oil		Observations
		Power (%)	Consumption (%)	
Anhydrous ethanol and diesel oil (%)	7 ethanol 93 diesel	−4.4	−2.4	Between 0°C and 4°C the mixture is not homogeneous (2.5% of ethanol separates).
	3.5 ethanol 96.5 diesel	−0.7	−0.8	Homogeneous mixture at temperatures over 0°C.
Anhydrous ethanol gasoline (and diesel oil) (%)	4.5 ethanol 4.5 gasoline 91 diesel	−2.6	−0.4	The maximum of mixture allowed without alteration in the motor is 10% (5% ethanol + 5% gasoline). The mixture has to be in the same proprotion.

Anhydrous ethanol vegetable oils and diesel oil (%)	33.3 ethanol 33.3 castor oil 33.3 diesel	−35	+59	Chemically homogeneous mixture.
	80 ethanol 20 castor oil	−20	+38	2-stroke diesel motor from Detroit Diesel Allison of Brazil.
Diesel oil and vegetable oils	Intol 220 (diesel + soy bean oil)	+1.5	+1.0	Other vegetable oils are being studied. The utilization of vegetable oil requires economic, agricultural, social and ecological studies.
	Intol 420 (diesel + babassu oil)	+1.6	+3.4	
Diesel oil, ethanol and additives (%)	7 ethanol 1.25 iso-amylic alcohol 91.75 diesel	−2.6	−0.4	Other additives are being researched by industries.
	10 ethanol 2 octylic alcohol 88 diesel	−5.7	+3.4	Research is under way.

Source: STI of the Ministry of Industry and Commerce, *Brazil Trade and Industry* (1980), Vol. 3, No. 9.

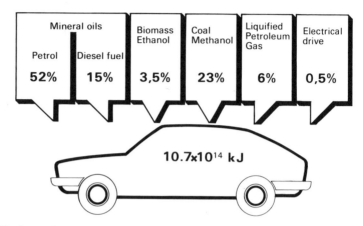

Fig. 5.1 Possible sources of energy for cars and combis in 2000. *Source*: VW Research and Development, Bernhardt, 1980.

methanol may come next. Figure 5.1 shows the main possible sources of energy in the year 2000.

All evidence seems to suggest that present engines will continue to dominate the automobile industry: spark-ignition (Otto) and diesel engines for automobiles and diesel engines for trucks. Within the engine itself, the basic components will probably not change significantly to improve efficiency, but engine operations will be closely monitored by sensors via integrated electronic systems to gather data for fuel/air mixture preparation, performance etc.

The internal combustion engine will therefore remain dominant for the next 20 years, because it is well developed and highly adaptable. The application of alternative fuels will require primarily engineering changes rather than scientific and technological breakthroughs. The technology for utilizing alcohol fuels and LPG in spark-ignition engines is well known and for diesel engines is under development. The main limitation for alternative fuels is likely to result from the economics of production of alternative fuels and their compatability with existing storage and distribution systems.

References

Automotive Engineering (1980), 'Gasohol—A 1937 view', **88** (2), 75-80.

Ibid. (1980), 'Fuel system adapts to varying alcohol content', **88** (2), 86-9.

Bernhardt, W. (1980), 'The alternatives and how to apply them to the world transport industry', *Second Montreux Energy Forum, 16-19 May.*

Bernhardt, W. (1980), 'Fuels from biomass', *International Conference —Energy from Biomass, 7-3 Nov.*, Brighton.

Big Farm Weekly (1980), 'Aussies ahead on fuel'.

Bôto Dantas, R. (1980), 'Production of alcohol: the Brazilian experience', *International Sweetner and Alcohol Conference. The Future of Sugar*, April, London.

Brazil Trade and Industry (1980), 'Vegetable oils, the new Brazilian way to save diesel engine fuel', **3** (29), 11-13.

Callaghan, J. M. (1979), 'Argument clouds gasohol issue', *Automotive Industries*, **159** (9).

Chambers, R. S. *et al.* (1979), 'Gasohol, does it or does it not produce positive net energy?', *Science*, **206** (4420), 789-95.

Eden, R. Q. E. (1980), 'Possible blending and marketing of alcohols as petroleum', *International Sweetner and Alcohol Conference. The Future of Sugar*, April, London.

Farm Chemicals (1980), 'Will you be selling gasohol in the '80s?', **143** (1), 42-52.

Hammond, A. L. (1977), 'Alcohol a Brazilian answer to the energy crisis', *Science*, **195** (4278), 564-6.

Hutton, R. (1980), 'Driving on drink', *Autocar*, 30 August.

Hall, D. (1981), 'Put sunflower in your tank', *New Scientist*, **89** (1242), 524-6.

Kampen, W. H. (1980), 'Engines run well on alcohols', *Hydrocarbon Processing*, **59** (2), 72-5.

Kane, E. D. (1980), 'The future of automobile's fuels and lubricants', *Automotive Engineering*, **88** (10), 37.

Ladisch, M. B. and Dick, K. (1979), 'Dehydration of ethanol, new approach gives positive energy balance', *Science*, **205** (4409), 898-900.

Lewis, C. L. (1979), 'Biomass is big but could be bigger', *New Scientist*, 1 February, 316-18.

Machine Design (1980), 'Corn states uncork gasohol gusher', **56** (6), 18-24.

Maura Leitâo, D. (1979), 'Etanol como fonte de energia, Programa Nacional de Alcool', *Brasil Açúcareiro*, **93** (1 and 2).

Scheller, W. A. *et al.* (1977), 'Gasoline does, too, mix with alcohol', *CHEMTECH*, 7, 616-23.

Volkswagen do Brasil (1980), 'Ethanol as an alternative fuel in Brazil'.

6 THE COST AND ENERGY BALANCE

6.1 Ethanol from Biomass Cost

Two major factors in the production of ethanol are its cost and energy balance. Any justification for the production of ethanol, at least in the medium and long term, must be based to a large extent on its economic feasibility.

The cost of producing ethanol depends upon many different factors such as the location of the manufacturing plant; the design, type and degree of modernization of equipment; the kind of raw material utilized; the relative labour costs represented; the scale of production and the total investment. There is no fixed 'alcohol cost' since it will vary between plants and even from day to day in the same plant. Unlike other raw materials weather conditions are also important. Energy crops with higher alcohol content per hectare do not necessarily result in the cheapest alcohol, for that will depend on exploitation costs. One of the major exploitation difficulties has been the ethanol producer himself since alcohol production was often linked to the petrochemical industry, being a by-product there also. In recent years undue control therefore was exercised over the relative prices of fermentation to petrochemical alcohol. This has been further complicated by the traditional tax that is applied to alcohol (ever since the times of the Pharoahs some 4000 years ago!) and despite the petrol tax (which can be high in some countries). These criteria must be borne in mind when making any assumption relating to cost and energy requirement or production (Tables 6.1–6.3).

As noted in Table 6.4, the development of new processes will play an important part in determining the cost of ethanol, and oil prices will soon be another important factor in the future.

Of all the costs (whether energy or money) the most significant in the ethanol production are those of the substrate and those of distillation from the low fermentation concentrations of about 10% to pure 100% alcohol. The latter can be further considered in two parts (again energy or money), the normal fractional distillation (rectification) from the 10% level to the eutectic point of 96% alcohol and the final dehydration of the 96% eutectic concentration to 100% pure alcohol. Whilst the distillation is energy intensive, the dehydration can be difficult and costly, particularly in terms of recovery of the dehydrating agent for recycling.

Alcohol can be dehydrated by using desiccants such as calcium oxide forming calcium hydroxide, but desiccants such as cellulose and cornstarch provide greater energy savings because less energy is required to dry them than to drive the water off calcium hydroxide. Another way of separating alcohol from water solution is a version of gas chromatography. Textile yarns such as rayon retard the movement of water vapours but allow organic vapours to travel freely. The water is removed by the yarn whilst the pure alcohol vapour is recovered from the other end of the tube through which the yarn is introduced. Alcohol dissolves readily in certain organic liquids, for example benzene, which do not mix with water. By exploiting this solubility difference alcohol can be recovered from aqueous solutions by solvent extractions. One version of the process uses a so-called 'critical-fluid'—a gas that has been compressed to the point where the distinction between gas and liquid disappears. At 50–80 times atmospheric pressure carbon dioxide becomes a 'critical' fluid and can be used to extract alcohol from fermentation beers that have been filtered to remove the solids. By this process the energy cost of the whole extraction process is estimated to be about 40–60% of the alcohol fuel value. Removing water from alcohol remains a serious problem since it is often argued this process consumes more energy than is contained in the fuel itself.

Another way of reducing energy requirements is to increase the fermentation ethanol concentration, 40–90 g per litre, with conventional technology. For example, some yeasts have been found capable of fermenting at concentrations of 250 g per litre albeit for short periods. A fermentation broth containing 200 g per litre ethanol requires little more than half the energy needed for distilling 40 g per litre. A broth containing this high level of ethanol requires a carbohydrate feed of 400 g per litre which imposes yet another need for new technology because of the starch separation. Thus improvements in alcohol fermentation— particularly water separation, will be important in the economics of alcohol.

6.2 Raw Material Costs

Looking at current processes the cost of raw materials represents 50% or more of the current total cost of ethanol produced. The remaining costs may be, roughly, split equally between fermentation, distillation and handling disposal of residues. For fermentation the major cost is the capital related charge associated, in conventional processes, with the large capacity required. The cost of both fermentation and distillation are greatly dependent on the alcohol concentration that can be achieved in the beer going forward to distillation without the loss of productivity.

Presently, sugarcane appears the most favourable. If, for example, the 'world price' of raw sugar (the major source of ethanol) is compared with 'world price' of crude oil, current costs display a relationship which is very favourable to sugar as an alternative raw material. But it is well known that the world price of raw sugar bears only a marginal relationship to the real cost of production. As for wheat, Stone and Webster have prepared a cost estimate for any ethanol plant using wheat feedstock in the Third World, of 100000 tons per year and concluded that its cost is some three times the price of gasoline, on an energy basis (see Table 6.1). In Brazil in 1977 terms, on an energy content basis, alcohol was fives times more expensive to produce than gasoline was in the US. But because of recent dramatic oil price increases and strategic considerations this has almost been reversed. Capital investment cost is also a major factor. Traditional sugar mills or

Table 6.1 Fuel ethanol production costs: basis and assumptions

Case	A	B	C	D	E	F
Location	Brazil	USA	Europe	Europe	Europe	Europe
Feedstock	Sugarcane	Maize	Wheat	Sugarbeet	Sugarbeet & green crops	Woodwaste
Status	Proven	Proven	Development	Development	Development	Research
Hourly capacity (t/h)	10	10	10	10	10	10
Operating (hrs/a)	5040	8000	8000	4320	7200	8000
Annual capacity (t/a)	50400	80000	80000	43200	72000	80000
Fermentables (wt/%)	14	61	66	12	av. 12	38
(as carbohydrate)	Sucrose	Starch	Starch	Sucrose	Sucrose	Cellulose
Ideal carbohydrate: ethanol (wt/wt)	1.86	1.76	1.86	1.86	1.86	1.76
Yield % of ideal	84	82.5	82.5	88	av. 85	70
Feed: product (t/t)	15.8	3.50	3.23	17.6	av. 18.2	6.6
Feed unit cost ($/t)	10	100	200	20	av. 18	30
By-product (type)	None	DDG	Protein	Protein	Protein	Various
Quantity: product (t/t)	—	1.24	0.45	0.25	0.25	0.5
Unit price ($/t)	—	150	300	300	300	200
Fuel (type)	With	Coal	Straw	'Tops'	'Tops'	With
Via (conversion)	Feed	Direct	Biogas	Biogas	Biogas	Feed
Fuel use (product/t (dry)/t)	—	1.00	0.425	0.4	0.2	—

	A	B	C	D	E	F
Fuel unit cost ($/t(dry))	—	40	35	20	20	—
Export electricity (kWh/t)	None	1000	660	600	600	1000
Unit price (¢/kWh)	—	3.0	5.0	5.0	5.0	5.0
Water + chemicals ($/t)	6	5	6	6	6	20
Fixed capital ($ million)	35	50	55	50	50	80
Production cost						
Feed	158	350	646	352	328	198
Fuel	—	40	15	8	4	—
Water + chemicals	6	5	6	6	6	20
By-product credit	—	186	135	75	75	100
Electricity credit	—	30	33	30	30	50
30% p.a. × fixed capital	208	188	206	347	208	300
Total $/t	372	367	705	608	441	368
Total ¢/litre	29.8	29.4	56.4	48.6	35.3	29.4

Notes: A = Sugarcane cost at $10/ton covering also disposal of stillage cost. The plant is assumed to be self-supporting in Steam and Electricity. Estimated capital cost $35 million for 10 ton/day/210 days/yr.

B = Fuel is assumed to be coal.

C = It is assumed that only a protein-rich fraction separated from the digester effluent is sold as a by-product.

D = Development status refers to the inclusion of an anaerobic digestion step.

E = A more speculative example assuming a successful development of a system of crops and farm management which supplies a succession of sugar-rich leafy crops on a regular basis during most of the summer, and at a unit cost slightly below that of beet.

F = Assumed some significant advances over established methods of hydrolysis of wood in respect of ethanol yield, and consumption of fuel and chemicals. Capital cost is regarded to be 60% higher than for cases B to E.

Source: S. R. Martin, The production of fuel ethanol from carbohydrates, Stone & Webster Engineering Ltd.

factories have had long lives, often over 50 years or more, but with the new processes now being introduced there is likely to be a stage of rapid development. As a result the rate at which capital plant is written off will be much greater than has so far been the case, and could become a major factor in the overall cost. It is often stated that biomass will become competitive as oil prices rise, but this is not necessarily the case, since during the initiation of such new schemes the major capital and operating costs will reflect the present cost of energy derived from oil, therefore it will not become independent of oil cost until biomass itself contributes to the energy for the complete manufacture of the biomass system.

The value of energy, of course, is very much a function of how it is presented—place, time convenience, cleanliness, continuity of supply etc., but in any case if a plant producing synthetic liquid fuel is to increase the supply of energy in convenient liquid form, the capacity of performance of the plant must therefore be measured by the net liquid fuel production and not by the gross production. Thus in calculating the capacity of a synthetic fuel plant and its costs, care must be taken to debit against production the energy required in the operation of the plant.

The economics of production of agrichemicals continue to be subjected to much debate since, as we have said, the cost can vary so enormously due to the variable factors which include delivery of raw materials, marketing, and distribution of end products. The following figures show the possible yields of final chemical products if each were produced exclusively from a 50000 ton/year ethanol feed:

	ton/year
Acetaldehyde	43500
Acetic acid	39500
Ethyl acetate	32500
Ethylene	29500
Polyethylene	28500
PVC	57000

Where carbohydrates are considered as feedstock for the traditional chemical industry processes they are at a disadvantage since these processes are based on a hydro-carbon feedstock. Hence carbohydrates must either be converted into conventional raw materials, or new techno-logy and products must be developed which use the particular properties of carbohydrates. Thus ethanol can readily and cheaply be converted into ethylene in a high yield (96%) by well-established technology using a process of catalytic dehydration with alumina at 350°C. Carbohydrates can provide a direct route to ethylene. Approximately 1.7 kg ethanol are required to produce 1 kg of ethylene. Since the theoretical conversion of carbohydrate into ethanol is around 50%, in practice about 3.7 kg fermentable sugars are required per kilogram of ethylene. Thus without allowing for pro-cessing or capital costs, at $0.31 per kilogram of ethylene (mid-1979 price) carbohydrates would have to be available at below $0.09 per kilogram (see also Table 6.1). Allowing for capital and production costs, to the best of our know-ledge, for ethylene derived from fermentation ethanol to be competitive at current prices the fermentable sugars would have to cost at the most $0.02 per kilogram. Hence ethylene prices would have to reach $0.79 per kilogram—equivalent to oil at around $45 a barrel—before ethylene from fermentation alcohol (at mid-1979) prices becomes an economic proposition. In monetary terms, it has been said, ethanol cost 75% more than petrol (in 1979) and the price of biologically-made ethanol would have to fall by 70% to make ethylene competitive.

Nevertheless it should be stressed that price considerations are not clear cut and there are many discrepancies as to the level at which it will be fully competitive with petroleum.

The Brazilian Government has argued that alcohol should be competitive at $25 + barrel, but it does not take into account subsidized interest rates and is doubtless an over optimistic assumption.

In an excellent recent book review entitled 'Biological Energy Resources', Slesser and Lewis (1979) have quoted the following Australian figures for the economic costs of photobiological fuels and prices of fossil fuels (Tables 6.2 and 6.3). Credit for by-products are also included. The conclusion was that on a $ per GJ basis liquid and gaseous

Table 6.2   Energy costs and efficiencies of photobiological fuels

Fuel	Raw material	Process	GER (MJ/kg product)	(GJ/ha/a)
Alcohol	Cassava tops[1] and tubers	Enzyme hydrolysis/ batch fermentation	17.3	+80
Alcohol	Eucalyptus	Acid hydrolysis/ batch fermentation	105.0	−452
Alcohol	Eucalyptus	Enzyme hydrolysis/ batch fermentation	>105.0	<−452
Methane	Cereal straw	Anaerobic digestion	20.0	+7
Methane	Eucalyptus	Anaerobic digestion	20.0	+84
Pyrolytic oil/Char	Cereal straw	Flash pyrolysis	4.8	+11
Pyrolytic oil/Char	Eucalyptus	Flash pyrolysis	4.8	+131

Source: Slesser and Lewis, 1979, p. 112.
Note: [1] It is assumed that the cassava cellulose tops can be burnt to provide most of the process steam.

photobiological fuels would be more expensive than the 'syn-fuels' from coals and even more so when contrasted with crude oil and natural gas at 1978 prices.

However, once again the geographical position of the plant, the political scene and availability of raw materials are not considered and these could alter economics drastically.

6.3 The Brazilian Scene

For ethanol derivatives Brazil subsidizes the price of ethanol if such derivatives replace a petrochemical based imported product (based on imported oil). This subsidy is 35% per litre of the price of ethylene per kilogram. In order to keep a price parity subsidies must fluctuate continuously according to price fluctuations of other equivalent petroleum products. Thus in the short term, at least, its success will be greatly determined by government's support. Table 6.4 shows the economics of alcohol production in Brazil from cassava and sugarcane distilleries of the same daily capacity (150 m^3/day). Total investment estimates vary none the less. The alcohol costs were computed assuming a return on

Table 6.3 Economic costs of photobiological fuels and prices of fossil fuels (1975 figs)

Fuel	Raw material	Process	Saleable by-products		Cost ($/t)	Cost ($/GJ)	Net energy (GJ/ha)
			As fuel	Other			
Alcohol	Cassava tops and tubers	Enzyme hydrolysis, batch fermentation	—	Fibre (animal feed); fusel oils	250	8.4	+80
Alcohol	Eucalyptus	Acid hydrolysis, batch fermentation	—	—	400	13.4	−452
Alcohol	Eucalyptus	Enzyme hydrolysis, batch fermentation	—	—	600	20.1	−452
Methane	Cereal straw	Anaerobic digestion	—	Biomass slurry	235	4.2	+7
Methane	Eucalyptus	Anaerobic digestion	—	Biomass slurry	310	5.5	+84
Pyrolytic oil	Cereal straw	Flash pyrolysis	Char	—	75	3.3	+11
Pyrolytic oil	Eucalyptus	Flash pyrolysis	Char	—	100	4.3	+131
Alcohol		Non-biological chemical synthesis	—	—	275	9.3	?

Source: Slesser and Lewis, 1979, p. 133.

Notes:

Fossil fuels (1975 costs)	Cost ($GJ)
Kuwait crude oil	1.25
Syncrude from coal	1.2–1.9
Petrol (taxed)	4.45
Diesel Fuel (untaxed)	2.0
No.6 Fuel oil	1.7
Natural Gas	1.15

Table 6.4   Economics of production of anhydrous ethanol from cassava and sugarcane

	Cassava hypothetical distillery		Sugarcane distillery	
Investment ($ $\times 10^6$)				
Fixed investment		15.8		13.3
Working capital		1.2		2.2
Composition costs	$/m³	(%)	$/m³	(%)
Feedstock:				
Cassava roots at $33.3/ton[1]	228	60.1	–	–
Sugarcane at $13.6/ton[1]	–	–	204	57.0
Enzymes, chemicals and utilities	60	15.8	6	1.7
By-products[2]	(16)	(4.2)	(15)	(4.2)
Labour	13	3.4	15	4.2
Maintenance, materials, operating supplies, insurance and administrative expenses	18	4.8	25	7.0
Taxes[3]	15	7.0	24	6.7
Depreciation	32	8.4	49	13.6
Net operating profit[4]	29	7.7	50	14.0
Calculated cost as fuel FOB, Distillery	379	100.0	358	100.0

Source: Yang and Trindade, 1979.

Notes: [1] Includes value added tax (sugarcane) and social tax (sugarcane and cassava).

[2] Difference between the cost of direct application of stillage as fertilizer and the credit of sales of hydrated ethanol and fuel oil.

[3] Includes income tax and social tax.

[4] Return on investment of 12% per year, based on the annual sum depreciation and net operating profit, and 15 years operational life for the distillery.

Basis: 150 m³/day cassava distillery operating 330 days/yr. (49 500 m³/yr).

150 m³/day sugarcane distillery operating 180 days/yr. (27 000 m³/yr).

Exchange rate: Cr$18 = US$1.00.

investment of 12% per year. The total cost of cassava alcohol and sugarcane alcohol differs less than 10%. The fuel alcohol administered price at $317–327/m³ ($1.20–1.24/gallon) early 1979, is lower than the calculated costs for both cassava and sugarcane alcohol, which were in the range of $360–380/m³ FOB distillery.

However, Slesser and Lewis (1979) indicate that the respective costs of sugarcane alcohol and cassava alcohol are $501/t or $397/m³ ($16.8/GJ) and $550/t or $249/m³ ($18.1/GJ) in normal practice. They state that these high costs are only acceptable because of the high selling price of petrol in Brazil $470/m³ ($19.9/GJ) and further comment that the impact of fermentation alcohol is purely political i.e. if the government set the ethanol price (1977) at $339/m³ ($14.3/GJ) then a profit can be made. As always these are 'historic' situations and economics. Slesser and Lewis (1979) admit time could radically change these relative costs both in terms of labour production costs, new plant technology and higher petroleum prices.

In Table 6.5 the cost of breakdown for an ethanol plant with a capacity production of 60000 litres per day is shown. As can be seen 56.57% of the total costs correspond to the raw materials and 14.78% to depreciation. The alcohol cost per litre was $0.30 in early 1979.

6.4 The Energy Balance

Any discussion of the feasibility of alcohol fuel or feedstock must necessarily take into account the net energy balance, the net liquid fuel balance and production costs. The most essential requirement in the production of an energy crop will be a positive energy balance. This is termed the Net Energy Ratio (NER) which is the ratio of energy input for growing, transporting and processing the crop. Numerous values for the NER of a variety of crops have been published, but each one reflects specific situations where they have been done.

Whilst the alcohol yield per hectare for the different crops offers no calculation problems, controversy remains on the question of whether production of ethanol from crops yields

Table 6.5 Cost breakdown for an alcohol plant with a production of 60 000 litres per day

Item	Cr$/litre	%
Variable costs		
Raw material	3.10	56.57
Chemical additives	0.16	2.92
Fuels and lubricants	0.02	0.36
Direct labour	0.07	1.28
Social security	0.04	0.73
Financial costs	0.13	2.37
Others	0.07	1.28
Fixed costs		
Indirect labour	0.34	6.20
Administration	0.07	1.28
Social security	0.20	3.65
Depreciation	0.81	14.78
Amortization	0.27	4.93
Maintenance	0.08	1.46
Insurance	0.08	1.46
Others	0.04	0.73
Total	5.48 (= 0.30 US$)	100.00

Source: Gochnarg, 1979.
Exchange rate 1 US$ = 18 Cr$.

a net energy gain. If there is an energy loss, regardless of its economic costs, the whole concept may have to be called into question no matter what the political considerations.

The controversy appears to arise from two distinctly different considerations, the energy consumed and produced in the process and the amount of liquid fuel involved. According to the US Department of Energy, to produce 100 Btus (105.5 kJ) of ethanol from corn requires the investment of 109 Btus (115 kJ) (44 Btu (46.4 kJ) to grow it and 65 Btu (68.6 kJ) to distil the alcohol from it), thus ethanol contains 8% less energy than invested in its production. But if by-products of distiller's grain are included, (14 Btu (14.77 kJ)) then there is a 5% gain. Further, if the corn is processed in

a petroleum-fired distillery and if most of the energy consumed in producing the corn is in the form of oil, the gain
will be small, if any. However, if the distillery is fuelled by
coal or solar energy then at least 9–13.5 litres of liquefied
fuel would be produced for every one consumed. In addition,
if the fertilizer used on the corn is produced in a plant using
fuel other than petroleum, then the liquid fuel yield would
be higher. As things stand it seems that alcohol will give a
net energy gain only if high crop yields can be obtained
without intensive use of fertilizer and machine cultivation,
otherwise the energy consumed in producing fertilizer,
harvesting crops and distilling the alcohol might actually
exceed the energy content of the ethanol.

In the case of sugarcane in Brazil, the output-to-input
energy ratio of sugarcane to ethanol production systems is
far higher than say in the US for similar systems. However,
the situation could be different because bagasse can be
used to fuel the distillery and provides a major saving in
energy requirement. In terms of total heat energy, 100 tons
sugarcane is equivalent to 70 tons of coal, or 40 tons of oil,
and can yield 6.5 tons of ethanol. Each hectare can produce
between 35–90 tons of dry sugarcane annually. This combination of a high alcohol yield per hectare and a built-in
source of fuel to operate the distillery makes it the most
attractive energy source at the present time. However, the
NER of producing alcohol from crops can be affected by
many external factors such as distance, market situation,
value of its by-product and the write-down value of the
distillery, because newly designed distilleries can significantly
improve this ratio.

6.5 The Case of Brazil

Da Silva and others (1978) have carried out an extensive
study of the energy content of ethanol production in Brazil.
Manpower, oil-consuming machinery, fertilizers, insecticides
and herbicides were translated into energy equivalents;
manual labour (a farm labourer) was translated into an
energy consumption 544 kcal (2.3 MJ) per week-hour.

The total weight of the farm equipment required for the

production of one hectare of cane on a farm where high technology is used, was estimated at 0.5 metric tons. Since data on energy consumption for equipment fabrication and maintenance are not available in Brazil, data from Pimentel *et al.* for corn in US was used—1050000 kcal/ha (4396 MJ/ha). This energy component was calculated for ratoon cane, cassava and sweet sorghum, the energy equivalent being scaled down according to the weight of equipment used per hectare. The only cultural energy computed in the industrial stage was the energy necessary for raw material processing and absolute alcohol distilleries which is accomplished by steam generation.

6.5.1 *Sugarcane*

The calculations were based on a sugarcane plantation and the ratoon with yields of 103, 62 and 50 tons respectively— 72 tons average, equivalent to 54 tons/ha/year since plant cane is harvested 18 months after plantation and uses soil for two years and ratoon cane has a 12-month crop period. Energy is produced in distilleries by burning the crop residues and it was assumed that each ton of sugar produces 250 kg of bagasse with 50% moisture. From the industrial processes it was assumed a total production of 66 litres of alcohol per ton of sugarcane with a consumption of 5.5 kg of steam per litre of alcohol. See Tables 6.6 and 6.7.

6.5.2 *Cassava*

Assuming a root yield of 29 tons/ha and since the plant requires two years to yield, the average yield is 14.5 tons/ha/ yr. Cassava is harvested manually. Moreover the raw material from farm to the factory travels further (on average 20 km) due to the fact that yield/ha is lower than sugarcane.

The industrial stage, including extraction and hydrolysis of starch, alcoholic fermentation and distillation, requires 6.5 kg of steam per litre of alcohol. Alcohol production is assumed to be 174 litres per ton of cassava.

Table 6.6   Expended energy average in the agricultural phase of energy production from sugarcane, cassava, and sweet sorghum. On average, plant cane requires two years to grow, ratoon cane requires one year. Cassava requires two years in which to grow. From sweet sorghum one can obtain two crops per year, one being a ratoon crop.

Inputs	Sugarcane		Cassava		Sweet sorghum	
	Mcal/ha	%	Mcal/ha	%	Mcal/ha	%
Manual labour	158	2.86	273	5.31	52	1.29
Machines	850	15.41	400	7.77	625	15.58
Combustibles	2635	47.76	2654	51.58	1861	46.40
Nitrogen	1204	21.82	1111	21.59	1111	27.70
Phosphorus	78	1.41	146	2.84	88	2.19
Potassium	192	3.48	115	2.24	115	2.87
Lime	50	0.91	100	1.95	25	0.62
Seed	273	4.95	250	4.86	13	0.32
Insecticides	4	0.07	48	0.93	73	1.82
Herbicides	73	1.32	48	0.93	48	1.20
Total[1]	5517	100.0	5145[2]	100.00	4011	100.00

Source: Da Silva *et al.*, 1978.

Notes: [1] The totals, in megacalories per hectare per year are: sugarcane, 4138; cassava, 2573; and sweet sorghum, 4011.

[2] If stems are harvested and transported for steam generation this number will rise to 7723 Mcal/ha, since 2578 is the cultural energy expended.

N.B. Energy units on this table have not been altered. However, SI units have been inserted in the text discussion of this data in 6.5.4.

6.5.3 Sorghum

The agricultural yield was taken as 32.5 ton/ha for stems and 3.0 ton/ha for grain. Both products can be used for alcohol production with a total yield of 3165 litres/ha. This crop requires only 4 months to grow; a possibility for one ratoon crop is included with a yield of 20 tons of stems/ha and two tons of grain/ha. Each ton of sweet sorghum produces 280 kg of bagasse with a heat value of 1300 kcal per kg of bagasse. Energy consumed in the industrial stage is 5.5 kg and 6.5 kg of steam per litre of alcohol produced from stems and grain respectively.

Table 6.7   The energy balance of ethanol production

Crop	Agricultural yield (tons)		Alcohol product (litres)			Energy (Mcal ha^{-1} year^{-1})						
						Produced			Expended			Balance
	Per ha	Per ha year	Per ton	Per ha	Per ha year	Alcohol	Residue	Total	Agri- culture	Indus- try	Total	
Sugarcane	72	54	66	4752	3564	18747	17500	36297	4138	10814	14952	21345
Cassava	29	14.5	174	5046	2523	13271	–	13271	2573	8883	11456	1815
Sweet sorghum[1]												
Plant[2]				3165	3165	16648	11830	28478	4671	10100	14771	13107
Ratoon[3]			4	2000	2000	10520	7280	17800	3350	6400	9750	8050
Total	62.5	62.5		5165	5165	27168	19110	46278	8021	16500	24521	21757
Sweet sorghum[5]												
Plant	32.5	32.5		2145	2145	11283	11830	23113	4671	6508	11179	11934
Ratoon	20.0	20.0		1320	1320	6943	7280	14223	3350	4005	7355	6868
Total	52.5	52.5		3465	3465	18226	19110	37336	8021	10513	18534	18802

Source: Da Silva et al., 1978.
Notes: [1] Stem plus grains.
   [2] Stems, 32.5 ton/ha; grains, 3.0 ton/ha.
   [3] Stems 20 ton/ha; grains, 2 ton/ha.
   [4] Stems 66 litre/ton; grains, 340 litre/ton.
   [5] Stems only.

6.5.4 *The Balance*

The expended energy requirement in the agricultural phase of energy production of these products is conveniently represented in Table 6.6. Sugarcane requires 5517 Mcal/ha (23 100 MJ/ha), cassava 5145 Mcal/ha (21 540 MJ/ha) and in the case of sweet sorghum 4011 Mcal/ha (16 793 MJ/ha). Table 6.7 summarizes the energy balance of ethanol production (industrial as well as agricultural stages), the energy produced and the net energy paid according to Da Silva's data, of 21 345 Mcal(89365 MJ)/ha/year using sugarcane— or 1.43 times the total energy consumed. Sweet sorghum has a net gain of 21 757 Mcal(91 090 MJ)/ha/year or 0.89 times the total energy consumed.

The ratio between energy produced from ethanol and energy consumed in the agricultural stage of sugarcane is 4.53, cassava 1.71, and in the case of sweet sorghum its net gain is 1.89 for grain plus stems and 2.01 if stems are counted only.

It must be emphasized that the data of Da Silva is regarded, generally, as optimistic since it might depend not only on the use of crop-residues but also on the low fossil-fuel energy costs of agriculture in Brazil. They neglect, for instance, the energy cost of manpower—although it is often considered more appropriate not to include manpower as an energy cost when re-evaluating other costs.

Moreira *et al.* (1979) utilizing the concept of a self-sufficient hectare, reach different conclusions. The 'self-sufficient' hectare consists of the partial utilization of an hectare for eucalyptus crop sufficiently large to cover the energy deficit on the industrial processing of the raw material grown on the rest of the hectare. For instance, for the sugar-cane crop (System 2 which is shown on Table 6.8) of which all the bagasse is used as raw material including cellulose, there is an industrial energy deficit which is covered by wood cultivated in 0.25 ha for each 0.75 ha of raw material harvested. As seen from the table, without the 'self-sufficient' hectare the net energy balance will be negative for sugarcane and sweet sorghum. For cassava it is in both cases negative. The energy needed for industrial processing is based on

Table 6.8 Energy balance: all the energies in Mcal per self-sufficient ha per year

Crop	Fraction of occupied area (%)[1]	Alcohol energy	Industrial energy			Agricultural energy			Alcohol energy[5] external energy	Total energy[6] external energy
			Produced[2]	Consumed	Balance	A[3]	B[4]	A+B		
Sugarcane										
System 1[7]	100	18020	23182	14704	+8478	3796	0	3796	4.75	6.98
System 1+2[7]	75	18558	4050	17612	−13562	2847	138	2985	6.22	6.22
Cassava										
System 1	81	10332	0	9964	−9964	1969	105	2074	4.98	4.98
System 1+2	79.8	11985	1440	12164	−10724	2976	110	3086	3.88	3.88
Sweet sorghum										
System 1	100	26114	26455	22585	+3870	7316	0	7316	3.57	4.10
System 1+2	65.7	23769	5155	23436	−18280	4829	187	5016	4.74	4.74

Eucalyptus										
System 2	87.4	12373	9439	16158	-6714	481	70	551	22.46	22.46
Methanol	72.8	18407	0	14773	-14774	401	150	551	33.41	33.41
Pinus										
System 2	84.8	16464	13432	21494	-8062	403	84	484	34.02	34.02
Methanol	68.3	21362	0	16798	-16798	322	175	497	42.98	42.98

Source: Moreira, J. R. *et al.*, 1979.

Notes: [1] Fraction of total area occupied by the crop. The remaining part is occupied by the eucalyptus culture, with the purpose of supplying the energy deficit of the industrial phase.

[2] Total energy extracted from available residues (bagasse or lignin).

[3] Energy consumed in the agricultural phase for raw material production.

[4] Energy consumed in the agricultural phase for eucalyptus production which is used as fuel in order to cover the industrial energy deficit.

[5] Only energy expended in agriculture must be computed as external energy. Industrial energy is supplied by wood and/or residues.

[6] Total energy = alcohol energy plus the remaining residues energy.

[7] System 1: Fermentation of sugarcane or cassava roots or stems and grains from sweet sorghum. System 2: Hydrolysis of cellulose from sugarcane, from cassava stems, from sweet sorghum and from wood.

burning eucalyptus—produced as a complement of the crop raw material. The last two columns of the table should be interpreted as follows:

1 The utilization of wood as raw material is 3–5 times more efficient than the other crops considered;
2 Wood is 50% more efficient if the final product is methanol.

6.6 Gasohol Energy Balance (Chambers, R. S. *et al.*, 1979)

The major technical advantages and disadvantages of utilizing ethanol as fuel were briefly analyzed above. As far as the energy balance is concerned, existing differences of opinion derive primarily from variations in energy assumptions and their interpretation. For instance any result is strongly dependent on assumptions about use of crop residues for the fuel and the miles per gallon rating of gasohol. Part of the controversy appears to have begun when Reilly calculated that the energy content of ethanol produced from farm crops is less than the fossil-fuel energy consumed in the process. It should be noted that excluding the positive energy balance given by Da Silva *et al.* (1978) most studies show little real net energy gain, if any.

In terms of total non-renewable energy, gasoline is noted to be closer to the energy break even point. In terms of petroleum substitutable energy, gasohol is an ambiguous energy producer, since most energy inputs to the process can be supplied by non-petroleum sources such as coal. The net energy balance is defined to be positive if the non-renewable energy requirement of producing gasohol to perform a specific task is less than the non-renewable energy cost of producing gasoline to perform the same task.

There is not any general consensus of this matter. Table 6.9 summarises the different options in the gasohol production, together with their quantitative effects on the energy balance. Scheller and Mohr (1977) assume that the crop residues like corn stalks and cobs could be burned in place of some process fossil fuel. For the case in which end-use efficiency is proportional to energy content, this assumption makes the difference between a net gain and a net loss.

Table 6.9 Energy balance in producing one gallon of gasohol from corn

| | (1 gallon) | Gasohol (0.9 gallons gasoline: 0.1 gallon ethanol) | | | |
		Reilly[1]	Scheller	ACR[1]	da Silva[2]
Fossil fuel joint					
Gasoline[3]	151kBtu	136kBtu	136kBtu	136kBtu	136kBtu
Ethanol	–	–	–	–	–
Agriculture	–	5	5	7	2
Process	–	14	17	5	4
By-product credits					
Distillers grains	–	–5	–5	–2	–
Crop residue	–	–	–12	–	–7
Net energy input	151	150	141	146	135
Fuel energy content	125	120	120	120	120
Energy balance	–26	–30	–21	–26	–15

Source: Environmental Science and Technology.

Notes: [1] As reported by R. S. Chambers *et al.* (1979).
[2] For Brazilian sugarcane.
[3] Includes energy content (125 kBtu/gal) and process energy (16 kBtu/gal).

Reilly's unfavourable analysis did not include the use of crop residues, though it did credit the full energy content of the distilleries.

Many of the options do not reflect changed technology but merely opinions on what factor should or should not be considered. On the whole Scheller and Mohr (1977), and Reilly refer to conventional distillation of ethanol for subsequent blending with gasoline, the ACR report refers to a new process that has been designed specifically to produce gasohol (not ethanol) with low energy consumption. Any ethanol production must rely heavily on the sale of the by-products; in any energy analysis the following must be assigned; all material outputs; energy output, all by-products and energy credit; although several energy 'penalties' may be subtracted from the energy content of the by-product.

For Chambers *et al.* (1979) an analysis assuming the use of standard agricultural production technique and conventional distillation technology leads to the conclusion that the net energy balance of gasohol production is negative. If, however, energy-conserving farming practices are developed and energy conserved by burning crop residues productively in the distillation process, it is possible to construct a realistic net of options with a modestly positive energy balance.

There are no simple answers to the energy balance and the controversy will continue depending on the basic energy source used. For example, Reilly's calculations put energy loss at 30 Btu (31.65 kJ) per gallon of gasohol. But this is not quite all the story, because it takes a net consumption of fossil fuel energy to produce a gallon of gasoline. The energy needed for refining amounts to 26 kBtu (27.43 MJ) per gallon and therefore this product of 1 gallon of gasoline —which has an energy content of 125 kBtu (131.87 MJ)— consumes 151 kBtu (159.3 MJ) of fossil fuel energy.

If an amount of ethanol which has an energy content equivalent to a gallon of gasoline can be produced with a consumption of less than 151 kBtu (159.3 MJ) the process is favourable, although the overall energy balance may be negative; but it must be less negative than the overall energy balance of gasoline production.

The energy content of a gallon of gasohol is 120 kBtu (126.6 MJ), slightly less than that of gasoline. A gallon of ethanol that has an energy content of 77 kBtu (81.23 MJ), and in terms of the yield of one bushel of corn, which is about 2.5 gallon of ethanol, is 192 kBtu (202.55 MJ). Whilst the energy balance in terms of gasohol facilitates comparison with gasoline, it obscures the energy balance of ethanol component, as the largest input by far is the 136 kBtu (143.5 MJ) per gal representing 0.9 gallons of gasoline. The energy content may however not be a true measure of fuel's efficiency in actual use. It shows that the energy balance is a strong function of end-use efficiency. If, for example, end-use efficiency is simply proportional to energy output, 1 gallon of gasohol would be needed to replace 0.96 gallon of gasoline; but producing that gallon of gasohol would require about 150 kBtu (158.24 MJ) of fossil energy as compared with 145 kBtu (153 MJ) per 0.96 × 151 for gasoline—a loss of 5 kBtu (5.27 MJ) for each gallon produced.

In summary it seems that the favourable balance reported by Da Silva *et al.* (1978) in Brazil may be due to the exceptional circumstances of that country such as the low labour costs. It is, therefore, quite possible that the total cost of sugarcane production is underestimated.

The technology employed in Brazil is currently basic, deliberately so, and thus technological improvements which improve alcohol production could probably tip the balance forward to a net positive energy balance. Perhaps, one should not worry too much about the energy balance since after all we require three times as much energy to produce electricity (as currently generated) mainly because the energy so produced is convenient, direct and transportable.

References

Arnold, M. (1980), 'Natural products, plenty more where that came from', *European Chemical News,* Technology Supplement, 22 December, 55-6, 58.

Büchel, K. H. (1980), 'Agricultural products, raw material and energy source of the future', *Chemistry International*, No. 5, 17-25.

Chambers, R. S. *et al.* (1979), 'Gasohol, does it or does it not produce positive net energy?', *Science,* **206** (4420), 789-95.

Chemistry International (1980), 'Biotechnology opens route from biomass to fuel', No. 2, 6-8.

Clock, G. (1980), 'Gasohol is it a plus or minus in the U.S.?', *Oil and Gas Journal,* **78** (9), 19-24.

Coombs, J. (1979), 'Biomass—future developments', *Biomass for Energy Conference, (C-20),* Royal Society, July, London.

Da Silva, J. G. *et al.* (1978), 'Energy balance for ethyl alcohol production from crops', *Science,* **201** (4359), 903-6.

Environmental Science and Technology (1980), 'Gasohol does it save energy?', **14** (2), 140-1.

European Chemical News (1980), 'Ethanol from wheat costs three times premium gasoline', 10 November, **35**.

Gochnarg, I. (1979), 'The Brazilian Alcohol Programme', *Biomass for Energy Conference, (C-20),* Royal Society, July, London.

Greenfield, P. F. and Dicklin, D. J. (1979), 'The interaction between energy accounting and cost accounting in the production of liquid fuels from biological materials', *UNIDO Workshop on Fermentation Alcohol.* DOC FD/WG 298/17, Vienna.

Harling, F. F. (1979), 'Lowering the cost of ethanol', *Science*, **206** (4414), 41-2.

Humphreys and Glasgow Ltd. (1980), 'Agrosources chemical'.

Johnstone, R. T. (1980), 'Ethanol, an alternative to its use as fuel', *The International Sugar Journal*, **82** (974), 41-4.

Kelly, F. H. (1980), 'Cost control factors in the production of ethanol from sugar cane', *The International Sugar Journal*, **82** (978), 12.

Ladisch, M. B. and Dick, K. (1979), 'Dehydration of ethanol, new approach gives positive energy balance', *Science*, **205** (4409), 898-900.

Macrea, N. (1979), 'Oh Brazil. A survey', *The Economist*, **272** (7092), 20-1.

Moreira, J. R. *et al.* (1979), 'Energy balance for the production of ethyl and methyl alcohol', *UNIDO Workshop on Fermentation Alcohol*, DOC ID/WG 293/2, Vienna.

Pimentel, D., *et al.* (1973), 'Food production and the energy crisis', *Science*, **182**, 443-9.

Scheller, W. A. and Mohr, B. J. (1977), 'Gasoline does, too, mix with alcohol', *CHEMTECH*, **7**, 616-23.

Slesser, M. and Lewis, C. (1979), *Biological Energy Resources*, E. and F. N. Spon Ltd., London and New York.

Tyler Miller Jn., G. (1980), *Energy and Environment: The Four Energy Crises*, Wadsworth Publ. Co., Belmont, Ca.

Yang, V. and Trindade, S. C. (1979), 'The Brazilian Gasohol Programme', *Development Digest*, **17** (3), 12-24.

7 FOOD OR FUEL AND THE ENVIRONMENT

7.1 The Food Fuel Conflict (Bedell, 1980; Brown, 1980)

A criticism that has been made of energy crop programmes is that they could divert agricultural production away from food crops, especially in the Third World countries. The implications of such a shift in agricultural production merit serious consideration in a world whose food supply is precarious.

The Less Developed Countries (LDCs), who in 1969 imported 28 million tons of cereals, will have to import, it is estimated, 90 million tons in 1985. Their import bill for cereals increases by 20% every year says the FAO, and in 1979 the total was 17×10^9. In these countries the poorest strata spend 55–80% of their income on food, and over 500 million of their population are suffering from malnutrition. In Africa alone twenty-six countries face a food crisis.

The basic argument is that energy crop programmes in the Third World could (if badly planned):

1 Compete with food crops for agricultural land;
2 Compete for rural investment which might be used to raise food crops yield;
3 Use food as a feedstock for industry rather than food for people and their animals;
4 Compete for water supplies—fermentation requires large quantities of water—about 16 litres for each litre of alcohol.

On the other hand, energy crop enthusiasts have argued in return that:

1 Energy crops will be in *addition* to food crops;
2 Fermentation of grain crops leaves a valuable high protein

by-product which can be used as animal feed or as high protein supplement for people;

3 Energy crop programmes will reduce oil import bills and save foreign exchange—which might be used to buy necessary food on the world grain market.

Little serious study has been done to settle these arguments, although we have past examples of the impact of other cash crops on food production which might serve to produce some indications of the sort of problems to be guarded against when encouraging biomass programmes.

7.2 The Cropland Competition

The numerous national programmes to divert agricultural resources to the production of fuel-crops are occurring at a time when efforts to expand world food outputs are losing momentum. The potential claim of automobiles on food-producing resources is thus serious. This is shown on Tables 7.1 and 7.2. As can be seen, a typical US automobile (10000 miles/year at 15 mpg) will require the equivalent food consumed by over thirty-six persons in the LDCs and would require the processing of over seven tons of grain per year and 7.8 acres (3.16 ha) of land against 0.2 acres (0.08 ha) per person equivalent in the LDCs where the diet is poor and simple. Table 7.3 illustrates the area demand for the different energy-crops. It ranges between 0.14% ha per car (for algae) and 0.66 ha per car (for cassava). (These projections do not necessarily fully coincide with those from Table 7.1.)

As for gasohol, to provide a 10% mix of alcohol in a typical US automobile would require 1460 lb (662 kg) of grain. These calculations do not include the fuel utilized in the production of alcohol. To produce 10×10^9 gallon (37.85×10^9 litres) per year of ethanol in US would require 20 million acres (8.1 million ha) and it is estimated that the soybean acreage reduction will be over 28 million acres (11.3 million ha).

In Brazil and in other countries, where the cars are smaller and sugarcane has a high alcohol yield per acre, about 2 acres of land may be sufficient.

Table 7.1 1985 Projections of minimum post-harvest food losses in developing countries

	Durables	Perishables	Fish
Projected 1985 food production[1] (million tonnes)	472	302	
Estimated minimum overall loss (percentage)	10	20	
Projected minimum losses (million tonnes)	47	60	10
Estimated price/tonne (1976 US$)	165	25	225
Estimated loss value (US$ billions)	7.8	1.5	2.3

Source: The USA Academy of Sciences, Post-Harvest Food losses in Developing Countries. *Development Digest*, vol. 8(4) October 1980.

Note: Based on projections of food crop production in 1985 and continued losses and prices at present levels (1980). Figures are regarded as conservative estimates and value is approximately 11.5×10^9.

[1] Based on approximately 2% annual increase from 1976 FAO production reports and figures in the World Food Nutrition Study (NAS. 1977, Appendix A, Table 1) of approximately 75% of total durable crop production used for food in 1985. Also assumes the proportion of durables to perishables produced in 1976 (61:39) will hold for 1985, and that there are no improvements in food conservation.

As food production has slowed down, global food insecurity has increased, together with population increase. The world's cropland has also been reduced remarkably, some of the reasons being the continuing conversion of cropland to non-farm uses, excessive soil erosion, the rising cost of energy for farmers and diminishing returns of additional applications of fertilizers in agriculturally advanced countries.

Because agriculture is playing a key national role in Brazil and because more attention is being focused on it, after years of neglect in favour of industrialization the agricultural sector has been made a top priority for the Figueiredo Government since it came into office in March 1979. Agro-exports are to become the mainstream of Brazil's export earnings in the 1980s and should total over 7.6×10^9 in 1980. Naturally in the energy sector agriculture will be very important. The government plans to invest up to 5.5×10^9

Table 7.2   Annual per capita grain and cropland requirements for food and for automotive fuel

	Grain		Cropland[1]	
	(pounds)	(kilograms)	(acres)	(hectares)
Subsistence diet	400	(181.4)	0.2	(0.08)
Affluent diet	1600	(725.6)	0.9	(0.36)
Typical European automobile[2] (7000 miles/yr. at 25 mpg)	6200	(2812)	3.3	(1.34)
Typical US automobile[2] (10 000 miles/yr. at 15 mpg)	14 600	(6621)	7.8	(3.16)

Source: Worldwatch Institute, quoted in Brown, 1980.
[1] Based on average world grain yields in 1978, according to U.S. Department of Agriculture.
[2] Fuel use converted at 380 litres of alcohol per metric ton of grain.

Table 7.3   Area demand for the operation of one alcohol car during one year

Assumption: mileage 15 000 kilometres per year, fuel consumption 10 litres gasoline equivalent per 100 kilometres energy consumption 20% less than a gasoline car

Biomass	Fuel	Area ha/car
Sugar beet	Ethanol	0.42
Sugarcane	Ethanol	0.47
Cassava	Ethanol	0.66
Potatoes	Ethanol	0.56
Wood	Ethanol	0.55
Wood	Methanol	0.34–0.46
Algae	Methanol	0.14
Wood (hybrid poplar 30 t/ha year)	Ethanol	0.22

Source: Bernhardt (1980).

(including infrastructure, particularly transport systems). If Brazil is to meet its target of feeding the urban masses, ending food imports, increasing food exports and producing gasohol, the country will have to bring an extra 4.5 million ha (11 million acres) under cultivation annually. That means digging and planting an extra area the size of Holland every year.

This is bound to aggravate social conflict (already quite serious in many parts of the country) since land ownership concentration has been increasing. Thus land reform is becoming more urgent, although it is unlikely that the government will introduce it, in spite of the promises of the recently organised government party—PDS, which has placed agrarian reform as one of its priorities. Because the political power base of the military has been rooted in the latifundia, land reform becomes too sensitive a political issue to be confronted. It seems to be a reform few people take seriously, in spite of the pressure being exerted by the new radical sector of the Catholic Church. For that reason any increase in output will come not from increased productivity of the existing lands but by incorporating new ones into the productive system.

7.3 Implications in Brazil

If Brazil's goal of automotive fuel self-sufficiency is implemented, it will require 16.9×10^6 ha of sugarcane, land which could be used for food production.

The social and political ramifications of the new phenomenon will probably surface first in Brazil if the Proalcool objectives are achieved—as is indeed likely. The present plans will require by 1985 that over 10% of Brazil's cropland be shifted to energy crop production.

The potential impact of this change needs to be thought about with respect to Brazil's social and economic system which has a distribution ratio of 36 to 1 between the richest one-fifth and the poorest one-fifth, and in 1975 one-third of its population was living at subsistence level and 21% of all children suffered from malnutrition. The decision to turn to energy crops to fuel the country's growing car fleet is certain to drive food prices upward unless special measures are taken, leading to more severe malnutrition among the poor. Despite its vast land resources Brazil is a chronically grain-deficient country, grain imports in 1980 were estimated to be some 6.1×10^6 tons.

Although Brazilian officials claim that the production of energy crops will be in addition to rather than in competition with food crops there are already examples to the contrary. Round the big sugar producing areas and near the big cities land use has been shifted to energy crop production and in 1980 this problem came to the surface when Brazil was forced to import black beans from Mexico because bean cropland in the south had been turned over to sugar for alcohol production (Brown, 1980). Additionally, it must be noted energy crops compete also with agricultural investment, capital, water, fertilizers, farm management skills, agricultural credit, technical advisory service and other scarce resources. We are not aware of any attempt to examine this impact and develop policies to counter deleterious effects.

Alcohol fuel has a powerful appeal to motorists who bear the brunt of rising petrol prices and who feel vulnerable to possible oil supply disruptions. The political influence of automobile owners in Brazil should not be underestimated, since the people who own cars are the urban elite who also dominate the political power structure.

7.4 Alternatives

It is not difficult to understand the reason for growing agricultural energy crops, but care must be taken and proper policies adopted to actually produce alcohol-fuel in addition to and not in competition with food crops. There are alternative sources of alcohol which are not obtained at the expense of foodcrops, such as wood, organic waste, forage, crop residues, bacteria, algae etc. These possibilities should be investigated further. Attention must be turned to available biomass that presently does not feed humans. Nevertheless before some of these alternatives can be utilized the basic system of sugar to alcohol, gasohol and gasoline substitution, its organization, and infrastructure must be in place.

7.5 Environmental Impact in Brazil (Energia, 1979)

It seems quite obvious that the Proálcool is bound to have a significant impact on the environment, particularly the alcohol distilleries. For each litre of alcohol the distilleries will have, as effluent, 12–14 litres of high biochemical oxygen demand (BOD) stillage.

This stillage has a relatively low pH 4.5 to 5.00. The expected 50×10^9 litre of stillage is equivalent to a sewage treatment blend required by a population of 160 million people, or 1.5 times the present Brazilian population. The total stillage output in 1977 alone was 20×10^9 litres— equivalent to the sewage of 60 million inhabitants. It is its high content of soluble organics and inorganics which gives stillage a high pollution potential.

Several solutions have been proposed for the disposal of stillage, they include application as a fertilizer for surrounding fields, concentration by evaporation to facilitate transport to other areas for use as fertilizer, or animal feed; anaerobic fermentation with recovery of methane and carbon dioxide. This latter process can be expected to lower the BOD by as much as 80% and allow a large amount of the remaining effluent to enter the country's extensive waterway system. This stillage can be also utilized as a nutrient for the production of single cell protein. Figure 7.1 illustrates the main stillage recovery and utilization alternatives feasible under Brazilian conditions.

In the state of São Paulo, the most important sugarcane producer with two-thirds of the distillation, some seventy-six sugar and alcohol distilleries have a pollution potential equivalent to 2.02×10^6 kg BOD/day of which 1.79×10^6 kg BOD/day (88%) are produced by the different systems of production of the various industries. The rest (12%) or 0.24×10^6 kg BOD/day represents a pollution equivalent to that produced by 4.4 million people (see Table 7.4).

Efforts are being made to reduce this high pollution level by both the State and Federal Governments. It is widely

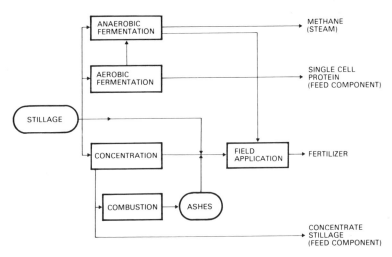

Fig. 7.1   Stillage recovery alternatives. *Source*: CTP multiclient study 'Stillage: technical-economic evaluation of process for stillage recovery as distilled by-product'.

known that with a much stricter legislation this level of pollution could easily be reduced without too many difficulties. The problem is that in a country like Brazil, as well as other LDCs, environmental considerations play a very secondary role. Whereas environmental problems in the industrial nations primarily circle around the notion of pollution, environmental disruption in the LDCs means something quite different: population growth and urban migration, slums and sewage problems, lack of fresh clean water. The LDCs are currently so engrossed in such problems that they pay little attention to the long-term issues. Generating employment and starting new industries are priority objectives.

Unless environmental awareness is consciously encouraged, effective change and measures will not occur. The LDCs do not have the capacity or the infrastructure or the experience to assess adequately the potential environmental risks. Because of the absence of monitoring agencies and the absence of environmental standards, coupled with the lack of ecological awareness, the governments of these nations are

Table 7.4   Potential pollution discharges and stillage from sugar-mills and alcohol in the State of São Paulo, May 1978

Place	No. of distilleries	Pollution discharges potential kg BOD/day		
		Potential	Stillage	Stillage (%)
Moji-Guagu	20	676942	73402	11
Capivari	5	98600	16195	16
Pardo	10	203880	27348	13
Piracicaba	15	395580	46891	12
Medio Tiete Inferior	12	406250	29335	7
Medio Tiete Superior	2	29640	650	2
Baixa Tiete	1	14193	438	3
Baixo Paranapanema	3	63079	5532	9
Alto Paranapanema	1	36810	3329	9
Iguapei Vertente Parcial	1	11400	352	3
Rio Grande	1	28500	19500	68
Turvo	4	52958	12690	24
Rio Sorocaba	1	16530	870	5
Total	76	2024382	236533	12

Source: Energia, 1979, p. 37, Table 14.

constrained. There is also an influential school of thought in LDCs which considers that environmentalism is an obstacle to economic development. This is particularly important in Brazil (a country which suffers severely from all these problems) (Bazin, 1981). Under such circumstances environmental impacts are likely to be responded to too late.

7.6 Gasohol Pollution

As noted, gasohol, generally speaking, is less polluting than other fuels. This is particularly the case in Brazil where blends may have a higher alcohol content than elsewhere and where cars may run on pure alcohol rather than gasoline.

Table 7.5 shows some test results found in Brazil. The

Table 7.5   Percentage of carbon monoxide (CO) in exhaust gases according to alcohol-gasoline blendings and air/combustible relationship

Relat. Air/Combust.	Percentage of CO		
	Gasoline	10% Alcohol	20% Alcohol
15.1	0	0	0
14.4	1.1	0	0
14.0	2.1	0.8	0
13.5	3.2	1.7	0.99
12.5	5.4	3.9	3.0
12.0	6.8	5.1	4.2

Source: Álcool Etilico, Avaliaçao Tecnologica, December 1978, Cat. CNPg-Table VIII–3, p. 326.

Note: Data based on tests taken in a Chevrolet six-cylinder engine. It shows that 20% of alcohol blend to gasoline, and a relation Combustible/air between 15.1 and 14.3 provokes a substantial reduction in hydrocarbons (HC) and (CO) but a considerable increase in NOx.

percentage of carbon monoxide in exhaust gases from 20% ethanol gasoline blend is 4.2% as opposed to 6.8% for pure gasoline.

If this data can be supported, then there appears to be some solid environmental considerations for supporting alcohol fuel. Although it appears to be a clean-burning fuel, it is not known whether exhaust emissions may contain poisonous aldehydes, or what will be the smell effects of a large fleet of cars burning alcohol fuel.

A secondary side effect in Brazil, is that given the incentives the government is offering to attract purchasers of new cars fuelled by alcohol, the overall number of cars may increase dramatically, increasing pollution and putting further pressure on the already overcrowded transport network.

A further unknown effect is that caused by spillage of alcohol. However, since it is soluble in water, cleaning up operations are considerably simplified. In Brazil most distilleries are near to rivers, and this considerably changes the risk.

One should now observe here the current controversy over the use of lead anti-knock agents in the petroleum-based First World countries. Clear indications of its effects are now beyond dispute. Not only would gasohol help to overcome this problem but a total ethanol basis in Brazil would prevent the repetition of past pollution problems encountered in cities like Los Angeles.

References

Bazin, M. (1981), 'Pollution by decree', *Nature,* **289** (5796), 342.

Bedell, B. (1980), 'The choice is not food or fuel, the Midwest strikes back', *The Futurist,* **14** (3), 27.

Bernhardt, W. (1980), 'Fuel from biomass', *International Conference, Energy from Biomass,* 4-7 November, Brighton.

Bowonder, B. (1980), 'Environmental management and the Third World', *Science and Public Policy,* **7** (3), 185-97.

Brown, L. (1980), *Food or Fuel: New Competition with the World's Cropland,* World Watch Institute Paper 35, Washington, D.C.

Carreras, M. (1980), 'Los cereales al borde de la guerra', *Cambio-16,* **468,** 89.

Chemical and Engineering News (1981), 'Gasohol focus shifts to effect on animal feed', **59** (3), 81-3.

Collombon, J. M. (1980), 'A more ecological agriculture for tomorrow?', *Impact of Science on Society,* **30** (4), 309-17.

Coombs, J. and Parker, K. J. (1979), 'Biomass, future developments', *Biomass for Energy Conference (C-20),* Royal Society, July.

Development Digest (1980), 'Post-harvest losses in developing countries', **8** (4).

Energia (São Paulo) (1979), **1** (5).

Gochnarg, I. (1979), 'The Brazilian National Alcohol Programme', *Biomass for Energy Conference (C-20),* Royal Society, July.

Lindeman, L. R. and Rocchiccioli, C. (1979), 'Ethanol in Brazil, brief summary of the state of industry in 1977', *Biotechnology and Bioengineering,* **21,** 1107-19.

New Scientist (1981), 'American automobiles turn to corn . . . but bacteria fuel the debate', **89** (1236), 132.

Ibid. (1981), 'How Brazil's gasohol scheme backfired', 16 July.

Ribeiro, C. C. and Castello Branco (1981), 'Stillage: a resource disguised as a nuisance', *Process Biochemistry,* **16** (3), 8-13.

Schwartz, R. (1980), 'Fuel from fields', *Showcase USA,* **2** (4), 10-15.

Trebat, T. J. (1980), 'Brazil: the miracle is over, but some good work may begin', *Euromoney*, April, **37**.

Yang, V. and Trindade, S. C. (1979), 'The Brazilian Gasohol Programme', *Development Digest*, **18** (3), 12-24.

8 THE BRAZILIAN EXPERIENCE AND THE THIRD WORLD

It is difficult to make any comparison between Brazil and the rest of the Third World Countries without analysing at least some of the major features. It will be almost impossible to present a comprehensive view here. We must be content to expose some of the major implications.

It is too soon to draw any final conclusions from the Brazilian experience so far, other than after 7 years it is still viable and on target. Certainly its success and errors will greatly influence many other programmes already underway or planned for the future, provide a learning experience for others who hope to follow a similar path.

8.1 The Biomass Alternative (LDCs) (Da Silva, 1980; World Bank, 1980)

In April 1980, a World Congress and Exposition of Bio-Energy was held in Atlanta (US) in which leading experts in this field from seventy-six nations took part. It is therefore fair to say that there is probably world-wide interest in this topic. Currently, only a few countries are actively involved at national level in obtaining ethanol from biomass, Brazil is, of course, a leading example. India, Thailand, Pakistan, Philippines, Sudan and South Africa are also giving serious thought to it: in the developed countries (DCs) Canada, France, Australia, New Zealand, and Russia are active. But by far the second most important, national effort—and with a wider implication—is the 'Gasohol Programme' in the US, albeit at an early stage of development.

The biomass alternative seems to be economically viable in special situations, particularly in tropical areas of Asia, Africa and Central and South America. The production of ethanol from local and natural renewable sources offers a great opportunity to reduce independence in imported petroleum, improving the balance of payments etc. For some nations such as those of the Sahel, an alternative to wood will be of extreme importance. For instance, in the Ouagadongon area (Upper Volta) it has been found that buying wood represents 20-30% of any family income. In Upper Volta, wood has to be carried to town by any means available from over 40 km away. In some surburban areas in Mali, the distances are frequently 15-20 km and even more. The importance of producing 'a green petrol' should not be underestimated in these particular areas of the world. However it must be pointed out that in these traditional areas many important changes in agricultural methods and attitudes would have to take place before such programmes can be implemented. If ethanol could replace wood, then this would be analogous to finding oil in Europe. It has been calculated that the annual family wood consumption in Upper Volta is in the order of 4.8 metric tons, this can be replaced by 144 kg of ethanol. (This calculation assumes that the wood is burned on an open fire and the ethanol is burned on an efficient stove.) Thus, sugarplant with a capacity of 30000 metric tons per year (presuming that molasses 90/100% for fermentation) would be able to produce sufficient alcohol to replace 80000 metric tons of 'cooking' wood (Moundlic, 1979).

As energy consumption increases in all LDCs (it is expected that it will grow at a faster rate than in DCs), new alternatives to traditional cooking methods are urgently required. By the year 2000 LDCs will account for approximately 25% of world energy consumption, a much higher percentage than they do now.

8.2 The Sucrochemical Industry in LDCs

Industrialization through the building of petrochemical units, has been the ambition, at least in the last two decades, of the LDCs. The energy crisis, the high level of investment required, the technological trends towards complexes of mammoth size which improve economics but complicate marketing, has destroyed this ambition, except for the few LDCs who are oil-rich.

Hence it is not surprising that attention is being focussed worldwide on the search for new sources of energy which are opening new vistas for the development of a chemical industry in countries with no, or limited, oil resources and limited markets, but with abundant water and solar energy which may allow them to produce ethanol on an industrial scale. The future prospects for an ethanol-based chemical industry in many LDCs are, therefore, encouraging if one considers that oil prices will continue to rise due to depletion of resources of supply. On the other hand, the potential of the agricultural products is only beginning to be tapped.

In our view there are many reasons to believe that, contrary to Brazilian practice, automotive fuel should play a secondary role in LDCs since those nations have more urgent and basic needs to fulfil. As we have already noted, it is their richer elites who really benefit from the automobile. Unless there is a surplus of alcohol or it is used as in a fuel in the agricultural sector, other needs such as cooking and chemical feedstocks should have priority since most LDCs will only be able to produce a limited amount of alcohol.

Most petroleum and chemical feedstock growth will be limited to the oil-producing nations, while the non-oil producing ones would have to concentrate on other alternatives such as coal, hydrogen, shale-oil, biomass etc. The most important chemical producing nations of today, such as US, Japan and Western Europe are expected to diminish in importance as petro-chemical centres as an increasingly weak feedstock position begins to erode the competitive position of these countries. This trend will clearly continue in the 1980s.

The LDCs should follow adequate policies to take advantage of these changes—and unlike Brazil which already has a strong petrochemical based industry, build an indigenous chemical sector based on renewable carbonaceous raw materials. Many of the LDCs are in fact seeing biomass as a potentially more significant source for organic chemicals particularly those which lack mineral carbon resources and finance to import them.

India appears particularly important in this respect since most of its alcohol production is directed to supply industrial uses—and not automotive fuel. There are *c*. 100 distilleries with an installed capacity of about 600 million litres. Total domestic consumption is 500 million litres (310 million litres for industrial uses, 170 million litres potable, 20 million litres for export). The alcohol-based chemicals installed capacity is over 116500 tons/year and new efforts are being made to study the growth of ethanol-based chemical industry.

It is interesting to note here that India, because of its closed economic system, has been able to operate a plant for many years which produces polythene from molasses via ethanol.

8.3 The Energy Crop Potential in LDCs (Hepner, 1979; Mariotte, 1979)

Chapter 2 dealt with Brazilian energy crops, but here we will outline some salient facts about energy crops and LDCs in general.

8.3.1 *Wood*

Worldwide production is *c*. 1.2×10^9 m^3 of which about 1.05 $\times 10^9$ m^3 is located in the LDCs. The importance of wood as an energy source in the Third World has already been noted —over-exploitation of forestry causes serious ecological consequences, thus if it is partially replaced by ethanol derived from other energy crops, it should bring important ecological benefits for those countries. It should be added, however, that in areas of poor rainfall, the growing of such energy-producing crops will pose problems since most of them require fertile soil.

8.3.2 *Cereals*

The world produced 1.46×10^9 tonnes of cereals in 1978, according to the FAO, of which 68 million tonnes were exported as surplus. The LDCs produced 426.9 million tonnes of which 27 million tons were also for export. But the major sources of surplus production are wheat and corn, mainly from the US and Canada, and therefore it can hardly be quoted as an important potential source of energy biomass in the LDCs.

8.3.3 *Potatoes and Sweet Potatoes*

The production is important but surplus of any significant amounts is scarcely found in LDCs. World potato production was 293 million tonnes of which only 27.7 million tonnes was from LDCs and of the 4.5 million tonnes available for export, just 0.77 million tonnes came from those countries. The only significant producers are: China (4.2 million tonnes), India (7.2 million tonnes), Turkey (2.9 million tonnes), Brazil (1.9 million tonnes). The production is mostly for food-consumption. Some countries such as Colombia and in Central America should be able to increase production well over domestic needs. The yield in alcohol is estimated to be 100 litres per tonne for sweet potatoes. World sweet potato production, in 1971-3, was *c*. 130 million tonnes per year of which 18 million tonnes per year was grown by Third World countries.

8.3.4 *Agrumes*

Agrumes (oranges, mandarines, lemons, grapefruit and other citrus fruits) production was 50.3 million tonnes of which 21.4 million tonnes came from LDCs who exported 2.2 million tonnes. Some of the LDCs are important producers, like Brazil with 7.6 million tonnes, Mexico 1.9 million tonnes, Argentina 1.4 million tonnes; and production could well be increased in many other countries. But alcohol yield is very low: 25 litres per tonne for pineapple and 35 litres per tonne for other agrumes. Conversion into alcohol might be a solution for rejected fruit or excess of production which cannot find an outlet in the World market.

8.3.5 *Bananas*

It is an important product for the Third World, which produced 54.8 million tonnes of the 56.5 million tonnes produced worldwide. LDCs are the major exporters (Brazil with 6.1 million tonnes, India with 3.9 million tonnes, Uganda with 3.4 million tonnes and Ecuador with 3.2 million tonnes are major producers in absolute terms). The yield of alcohol from this crop is good—c. 250 litres per tonne average (green banana 300–350, ripe banana 100–110 litres per tonne).

A million tonnes of bananas could produce 250 million litres of alcohol. The distillation could be made with the special preliminary equipment used for the distillation equipment for molasses and sugarcane. There is an excess of banana production in the world, and production could easily be increased.

8.3.6 *Cassava*

As seen above, this is an extremely important product, at least in Brazil. About 12.6 million ha are allocated for its production in the world with a harvest in 1978 of 110 million tonnes, 108 million tonnes of which came from LDCs. It is very much a Third World product.

8.3.7 *Sugarcane and Sugarbeet*

The importance of sugarcane was outlined above, not only in the Brazilian case but for other LDCs. If on the other hand sugarbeet is included then it is the world's most important single product. World production (1977) was c. 1028 million tonnes—735.5 million tonnes for sugarcane and 290 million tonnes for sugarbeets, of which the LDCs accounted for 619 million tonnes and 18.5 million tonnes respectively. Sugarbeet has not got much importance in the LDCs, whilst sugarcane, except for US and Australia, is predominantly a Third World crop.

In addition, sugar is produced in 110 countries (69 sugarcane, 31 sugarbeet, 10 both) and therefore has the other advantage in that there is a well-known and developed technology. There are 2496 sugar plants with over 400 tonne per day capacity in the world. Although expansion has been rapid in the last 10 years there is still a good potential for expansion around the world, with a relatively low investment.

8.3.8 *Molasses and Starchy Roots*

Their importance requires further elaboration. The total world production of molasses in 1975 was *c.* 27 million tonnes and the projections for 1985 are 33 million tonnes. Twelve major LDCs will be producing 12.8 million tonnes in 1985. Thailand, Brazil, Cuba and Philippines will be main producers. The amount of alcohol that could be obtained is expected to be 1.9 million tonnes.

The world production for starch roots (including cassava) was in 1975, 130 million tonnes (102 million tonnes of cassava) and it is expected to be 160 million tonnes by 1985. Brazil will occupy the first place with 36 million tonnes followed by Nigeria (30 million tonnes), India (20 million tonnes), Indonesia (17 million tonnes) and Zaïre and Thailand (with 12 million tonnes). If in 1985 excess production of sugar, molasses and starchy roots were converted to ethanol, it could yield 6.7 million tonnes of ethanol (2 million tonnes from sugar; 1.9 million tonnes from starch roots). Brazil and Thailand account for just over 40% of total ethanol potential from these products: Cuba and India for another 20% followed by Philippines, Nigeria and Zaïre. This potential availability of alcohol in various countries is shown in detail in Table 8.1.

There are, of course, many other less important crops such as grass biomass, which in the long-term may become important resources.

8.4 The Economic, Social and Political Setting for Ethanol Production

8.4.1 *Economics*

The LDCs are by no means uniform in their economic and social structures. Because their degrees of economic advancement and resource endowment vary widely, so does their actual and potential capacity to produce ethanol via the biomass fermentation route. We note, for example, the costs of producing sugar vary considerably between different sugar producers, in 1977 a ton of sugar cost $6–8 in Brazil and $13.7 in Nicaragua. Therefore, it is hard to generalize about

Table 8.1 Potential availability of alcohol from sugar, molasses and starchy roots 1985 (thousand tonnes)

	From sugar	From molasses	From starchy roots	Total
Central America and Caribbean	170	160	–	330
Argentina	75	25	–	100
Brazil	505	400	680	1585
Colombia	–	–	160	160
Cuba	660	190	–	850
Dominican Republic	125	25	–	150
Mexico	–	165	–	165
Total America	1535	965	840	3340
India	–	100	580	680
Indonesia	–	–	70	70
Philippines	165	185	–	350
Taiwan	55	25	–	80
Thailand	135	535	530	1200
Total Asia	355	845	1180	2380
Ghana	–	–	40	40
Ivory Coast	40	45	90	175
Nigeria	–	–	250	250
Sudan	70	75	–	145
Tanzania	–	–	150	150
Zaïre	–	–	250	250
Total Africa	110	120	780	1010
World Total	2000	1930	2800	6730

Source: Hepner, 1979, p. 23, Table 10.

the viability of ethanol production, one needs specific data and information for each potential producer. Nevertheless, Mariotte (1979) has tried to estimate the economic potential of ethanol production for LDCs located 30° north and south of the equator (excluding Brazil). The investment required to replace 15% of their petrol by ethanol would be around $10 $\times$ 10^9. Annual foreign exchange savings (which would be linked to oil prices) would probably be over $1.5 $\times$ 10^9.

Of course, detailed analysis might well show that there are only a limited number of countries which will meet all the necessary conditions (availability of land, adequate rain and sunshine, good soil and cheap labour supplies etc.) for the economic utilization of biomass energy as a primary source for their development. In many countries, however, it may well prove to be, to varying degrees, a useful additional energy source.

As in Brazil, the state would have to play a key role in the implementation of Third World national biomass programmes. Private finance would be unlikely to be spent on the necessary R&D programme and financial and other incentives would be required—at least initially—to encourage the substitution of ethanol for oil. Such programmes would call for clear government policies and commitment.

8.4.2 *Socio-Political*

Conditions in the LDCs stand in stark contrast to those of the developed industrial nations. They are not energy intensive 'economies as a whole—although some may possess energy intensive industrial sectors or regions—their per capita energy consumption is low and they currently use only a fraction of the energy consumed by the industrial nations, despite the fact that they contain far more people. Their environmental and energy situations are very different to those of the industrial states, and the types of energy technologies developed by the latter may well be inappropriate. Yet the flow of technology from the industrial to Third World states is overwhelmingly unidirectional. The Third World is becoming increasingly technologically dependent, and, since R&D is also concentrated in the industrial nations, will remain so. The global expenditure on R&D in 1973 was estimated to be $94.4 $\times$ 10^9, less than 3% of this figure was spent in the Third World. We could also say that this 3% approximates to the extent to which R&D is directed towards satisfying

Third World needs, that is the needs of the majority of the world's population (Norman, 1979).

Because the Third World possesses such meagre technical resources, in addition to their weak financial and structural resources, any natural advantages that they might enjoy for biomass energy potential could easily be wasted. Successful biomass programmes will require R&D appropriate for specific national requirements. Currently most Third World countries lack the capacity to develop a 'green technology' and most industrialized countries lack incentive. It looks as though this technology which offers most to Third World nations will need to be developed, in the main, by them. Therefore, the Brazilian PNA, seen from the perspective of an ever increasing trend towards Third World technological independence, assumes a special importance over and above its specific technical and economic content. Could it be a step towards the development of a greater degree of technology transfer between the Third World countries themselves?

8.5 The Lessons for the Third World

Despite the world-wide interest aroused by biotechnology, few countries are as yet fully committed, as is Brazil, to national programmes for biomass utilization. Furthermore, given the magnitude of the task, and the varying degrees of economic endowment and biomass resources amongst the LDCs it is not easy to make valid comparisons between Brazil and other LDCs on this question. First, because Brazil possesses special characteristics of its own: the absolute size of its biomass resources is unrivalled elsewhere in the Third World; and the unique historical agro-industrial experience upon which the PNA could build. Secondly, the PNA itself is still at an early stage of development and it is too soon, therefore, to pass more than a provisional judgement on it. The fact that Brazil, a Third World nation, has successfully established the PNA does not mean that its experience should be utilized uncritically by other Third World States wishing to establish their own biomass programmes.

The PNA itself has not been immune to political criticism, some of which has come from people who support the principle of a national biomass programme. They argue that the Brazilian Government, as chief decision-maker within the PNA—a centrally planned and state-initiated programme—often failed to consult properly with those parties most directly affected by the programme. They point out that the PNA's impact on land tenure has tended to increase rather than decrease the concentration of rural wealth, and that in the urban areas the gasohol programme can be considered to be a state aid programme for the car-owning middle classes—who are, relatively speaking, a wealthy elite. Thus, say critics, the PNA in its present form will on balance do little to reduce the massive social inequalities in Brazil, indeed it appears to be helping to maintain them.

Leaving aside such social and economic lessons that other LDCs might draw from the PNA, we should now consider what it could offer technically. Brazil, as we have shown, has amassed a great deal of experience with sugarcane as a substrate and has begun to examine, also, alternative substrates but these latter substrates are still at an early stage of development and are certainly not yet commercially viable. We must conclude that, in the short-term, the technology that Brazil could offer is probably limited to sugarcane fermentation technology. However, there might be mileage to be exploited by other Third World states and Brazil co-operating in joint research and development programmes on fermenting substrates other than sugarcane.

LDCs which do not possess indigenous reserves of fossil fuels face a most uncertain and bleak economic and political future. In order to reduce their national vulnerability to external suppliers of energy they will need to develop alternative energy sources derived from their own resources. The development and innovation of biotechnology to utilize biomass resources is likely to be an appropriate energy option for many tropical and sub-tropical states. Ideally, future Third World biomass programmes should be based upon realistic planning in accordance with satisfaction of basic needs; and carried out in a manner which envisages, and allows, greater socio-economic and structural changes, together with greater consultation and participation of the parties most directly affected than was the case in the PNA.

Steps would have to be taken to ensure, for example, that energy crops were additional to, rather than in competition with, food crops. Likewise such a programme, if it followed the ethanol route, might avoid utilizing the bulk of the ethanol for automotive fuel—as Brazil has done—preferring to concentrate on ensuring an adequate energy supply for agricultural and other rural uses.

The Brazilian Alcohol Programme (PNA) is a result of a combination of unique industrial, political, economic and technical factors. It is a sterling achievement that a Third World nation has shown that they are able to pioneer the development and application of biotechnology to satisfy national economic and industrial needs on a scale yet unmatched elsewhere. However, no matter how successful it may turn out in Brazil, it is not necessarily a model to be adopted uncritically. Nevertheless, it cannot be other than encouraging to the Third World that if the Brazilians can successfully succeed in this energy problem, they will help to destroy the myth that the nations of the South are doomed forever to progress along technical routes proved, and owned, by the North.

References

Abelson, P. (1980), 'Energy from biomass', *Science*, **208** (4450), 1325.

Brown, L. (1980), *Food or Fuel, New Competition for the World's Cropland*, World Watch Institute, Paper No. 35, Washington, D.C.

Chemical Age (1980), 'Constraints and innovations', 27 June, 22–33.

Ibid. (1980), 'Opportunities and constraints', 4 July, 12–13.

Coombs, J. and Parker, K. J. (1979), 'Biomass, future developments', *Biomass For Energy Conference (C-20)*, Royal Society, July, London.

Da Silva, E. J. (1980), 'Biogas: fuel of the future', *Ambio*, **9** (1), 2–9.

Fritz, M. (1979), 'Government responsibility in energy and environmental policies', *UNIDO Workshop on Fermentation Alcohol*, DOC. ID/WG 298/9, Vienna.

Hall, D. O. *et al.* (1982), *Biomass for Energy in Developing Countries*, Pergamon, London.

Hepner, L. (1979), 'Potential availability of fermentation alcohol from sugars and starches in developing countries', *UNIDO Workshop on Fermentation Alcohol*, DOC. ID/WG 293/33, Vienna.

Lebre la Revere, E. (1980), 'Consequences of the Brazilian Alcohol plan', *Ecodevelopment News* (13), 14-23.

Maisel, D. S. (1980), 'Trends in the chemical industry', *Chemical Engineering Progress,* **76** (1), 17-23.

Mariotte, P. (1979), 'Necessary conditions to promote and realise a policy for energy and chemical based on "green petrol" ', *UNIDO Workshop on Fermentation Alcohol,* DOC. ID/WG 293/24, Vienna.

Moundlic, J. (1979), 'Can fermentation alcohol substitute for wood as cooking fuel?', *UNIDO Workshop on Fermentation Alcohol,* DOC. ID/WG 293/28, Vienna.

Norman, C. (1979), *Knowledge and Power: The Global Research and Development Budget,* World Watch Institute, Paper 31, Washington, DC.

Sharma, K. D. (1979), 'Present status of alcohol and alcohol-based chemicals industry in India', *UNIDO Workshop on Fermentation Alcohol,* DOC ID/WG 293/14, Vienna.

The World Bank (1980), *Alcohol Production From Biomass in the Developing Countries,* Washington, DC.

9 THE FUTURE

9.1 Biomass in Brazil

The PNA programme is still in its early stages and its outcome cannot be predicted with any certainty. Yet already no-one doubts that it has made, and will continue to make in the future, a deep impression beyond Brazil's boundaries. Other nations, many also developing economies of the South, should attempt to learn from Brazil's experience with pioneering large-scale utilization of biotechnological conversion of biomass.

The PNA is opening up many new possibilities undreamed of just a few years ago and the outcome will depend on many different factors. Some of these can be taken care of within the PNA programme itself, however, others are external to it, and in a sense beyond the control of the PNA planners, e.g. the world energy situation. We expect to see important technical advances which will benefit the economic viability of alternative energy systems and new chemical feedstocks. At the social level, the PNA record and prognosis is contradictory; there have been positive achievements, however, as we have seen, they have been accompanied by the problems which will need correcting in the future version of the plan.

9.2 The Energy Scenario

It is not easy to foresee how the world energy situation will be in the short term, let alone in the long term. As for the PNA original objectives, it is quite certain that many changes will have to be made to adapt to planning errors and changing situations. This flexibility could be of extreme importance in the future.

Carvalho *et al.* (1979) have analysed and constructed

different energy scenarios up to 1988 (see Fig. 9.1). Their model was designed to incorporate endogenously the following factors:

1 Cracking flexibility of the three major petroleum derivatives, fuel oil, diesel oil and gasoline;
2 Technological levels and limits for alcohol mixtures (the maximum blend would be 20%, although 25% may be technically possible);
3 Different alcohol performances depending on its application;
4 An assumption of stable alcohol production.

Policy related parameters are left as exogenous inputs. The scenarios were developed to evaluate the impact of methanol and ethanol availability from 1979–1988. Ethanol is to replace gasoline and diesel oil, and methanol is to displace diesel oil and fuel oil. Ethanol availability corresponds to official estimates during 1979/80, whereas figures from 1981 onwards correspond to a 30% increase over the official estimates. For methanol the maximum availability corresponds to the introduction of one 2000 tons methanol-per-day plant every 2 years, commencing in 1982. Annual alcohol availability in 1988 is expected to be about 3.0 million m^3 of methanol and 6.5 million m^3 of ethanol.

Scenario I and II correspond to a relatively low increase in annual demand (3% for gasoline and diesel and 1% for fuel oil). Scenario II increases demand by 5%, 8% and 3.5% respectively. According to Scenario I and II about 760000 light vehicles should be operating on neat ethanol (Otto engines) by 1988—about 15% of the total automotive production during 1979–1987. The number of neat alcohol buses and trucks (using ethanol/methanol as diesel substitute) would be c. 55000 (an annual average increase of 5–7000 vehicles).

9.3 Types of Alcohol Fuel

Future fuels will be dependent on the favourable results of various alternatives now under study (vegetable oils, diesel substitutes etc.). The substitution of diesel by vegetable oil,

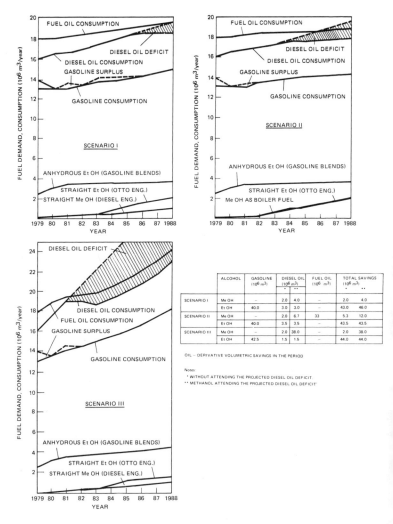

Fig. 9.1   Examples of alcohol fuels; scenarios, 1979–88. *Source*: Carvalho *et al.*, 1979.

as we have already noted, will be far and away the most significant achievement since diesel is so widely used in Brazil. The options currently under investigation for diesel oil substitution have already been described. These include the utilization of heavy gasoline blended with diesel oil, diesel engines powered by alcohol +10–15% ignition improvers, neat vegetable oil with up to 5% ignition improvers and blends of diesel oil with up to 4% alcohol, up to 60% alcohol plus additives, and up to 30% vegetable oil, including modified diesel engines using other varieties of fuel.

It should be stressed that these studies are in an early stage of research and, furthermore, it will be some time before any final assessments can be made. However, up to now the results are encouraging. Other studies include not only methanol as fuel for Otto and diesel engines but also for gas turbines and boilers. The experience of fuel alcohols in Brazil with gas turbines has been limited to the CAÇÕES and São José Campos stations and laboratory experiments.

9.4 Technologies and Feedstocks (Goldstein *et al.*, 1980)

The current situation of the several feedstocks under consideration can be summarized as follows:

1 *Sugarcane*—almost all ethanol produced from this crop. Large improvements are possible in the present agricultural and industrial technologies.
2 *Cassava*—the world's first commercial plant (60 m³ per day in Curvelo M.G.) is still in a pre-operational stage due partly to the lack of large-scale agricultural experience with this crop. Several additional industrial developments are needed to improve its economics. Ten new projects of ethanol from cassava are included in the PNA financing list.
3 *Sorghum*—no commercial plants are in operation in Brazil yet, nor are there any being carried out.
4 *Babassu*—no commercial plant is working at the moment, a 30 m³ per day project has been approved to start production in 1982/83.
5 *Wood*—no commercial plants available; however, there

is a lot of interest in it, particularly methanol from Eucalyptus wood. Technological problems still remain. A Government corporation—COALABRA—has been incorporated to implement wood alcohol.

6 *Sweet Potatoes*—(another potential crop in medium term). There are not yet any commercial plants.

Many technological and fermentation improvements are still needed, despite the many studies that have been and are being done. According to the *Centro de Tecnologia* biomass fuel alcohol progress technology in Brazil is likely to improve rapidly in the future in the following areas:

1 *Agriculture*—optimized for fuel alcohol crops.
2 *Industrial Conversion*—less energy consumption; higher yields; continuous processes; new separating techniques; vinasse (stillage) treatment.

9.5 The Medium Long-Term Problems

The PNA programme offers, as we have stressed throughout this report, many opportunities, from a national economic development viewpoint. For example: a large market for technology and equipment in the agricultural and industrial sectors; a growing independence from imported oil and chemical feedstocks.

At the same time there are many obstacles to be overcome. It requires: high investment; greater planning control; more R&D funding than has been the case so far; more equipment; the construction of more independent distilleries (so as to make alcohol supply less susceptible to international sugar price fluctuations); greater diversification of ethanol-based crops; far greater attention to be paid to possible environmental impacts. There should also be more emphasis on ethanol as an alternative feedstock than has been the case so far, particularly in those regions with alcohol market imbalances.

There should also be more resources available for new process technology (particularly for microbiological systems) that can, for example, efficiently convert cellulosic feedstocks into fuel ethanols.

9.6 The Lessons for the Third World

The example of Brazil has to be a powerful stimulus for all non oil-producing countries to consider seriously what their options are for developing energy sources of their own. That developing countries must develop their own national energy sources is beyond question when one compares their situation with that of developed industrial states.

The World Bank (1980) has graphically illustrated that comparison which is shown in Table 9.1.

Table 9.1 Per capita energy consumption in kg of coal equivalent (1975)

Low-income states	52
Middle-income states	524
Industrialized states	5016

The low- and middle-income states together contain a total of 127 states with over 2820 million people. As Mariotte (1979) points out:

'How will it be possible for developing countries to have the financial resources to import enough petroleum to meet their energy requirement, which is absolutely necessary to improve their living conditions, their industry and agriculture? Therefore, it is a *must* for them to find, in their own territories, alternative resources such as sugarcane, or cassava which help them to meet their energy requirements.'

With this in mind a UNIDO report stressed the following principles for successful Gasohol programmes:

— that the Government must declare biomass alcohol as a permanent source of energy within the national package of energy sources;
— that the Government should proceed to organize the production of the necessary biomass crops, build the necessary distilleries and alcohol distribution channels;
— that the Government should organize appropriate financial aid and incentives: encourage investments and obtain loans etc., from International Organizations etc., for equipping the country with distilleries and process equipment etc.;

fix an attractive price for alcohol as an incentive to those who are prepared to engage in oil substitution.

All of these principles have been adopted in Brazil and given added refinement within the PNA. The lessons to be learned from the Brazilian PNA experience are thus as much *political* as *technological*.

References

Carvalho, A. V. *et al.* (1979), 'Future scenarios of alcohols as fuels in Brazil', *Alcohol Fuel Technology—Third International Symposium,* 28-31 May, Asilomar, Ca., USA.

Goldstein, L. *et al.* (1980), 'Fermentation ethanol as a petroleum substitute', *15th Intersociety Conversion Engineering Conference IECEC '80,* August, Seattle, Washington, USA.

Trindade, S. C. (1980), 'Fuel alcohol, suitability of sugarcane as feedstock', *World Sugar Research Organisation Ltd. Conference,* 26-27 February, Stanford Court, San Francisco, Ca., USA.

Trindade, S. C. *et al.* (1980), 'Outlook of ethanol fermentation concentration technologies', *World Bio-Energy '80 Conference,* 22 April, Atlanta, Georgia, USA.

World Bank (1980), *Alcohol Production From Biomass in the Developing Countries,* Washington, DC.

10 UP-DATING SUMMARY

During the preparation and completion of this project and book, further new facts concerning the Brazilian situation have come to light, and are examined briefly here to provide further perspective to the Brazilian experience.

The Brazilian Government is slowing its energy installation programme due to the present economic situation. The world recession has hit exports and caused lower estimates of growth for the next two decades. Confirmation of this slow-down has been incorporated in the revised version of *PLANO 2000* (1981).

NUCLEBRAS, the State agency in charge of the nuclear programme, has recently put the cost of the programme at 24×10^9 almost double the original estimate. New revisions have been made and these include:

— limitation of reactors to the nine already planned with a capacity of 11 000 megawatts but completion date delayed 5 years later than originally planned (2000);
— only four of the original eight reactors are to be ordered from West Germany and these too have delayed commissioning dates;
— The Itaipu hydroelectric power plant shared with Paraguay on the Parana River will be delayed 18 months by stretching the time for installation of its 18 700 megawatt turbines;
— ten other smaller hydroelectric power plants to be delayed by 5 or 6 years.

The government policy for the PNA, the power alcohol programme, is also reflecting the slowing in economic growth and monetary policy. The 8% growth in the programme in 1980 has dropped to near zero growth in 1981 and this plus public's lack of confidence that the government would not maintain the programme has considerably hurt the Proálcool programme. The recession has hit harder than expected and industrial production has plummetted. Gasoline, a source of government revenue, began to be stockpiled. The Minister of Planning, Antonio Delfim Netto, declared that the subsidies for Proálcool were 'inflationary' whilst other government officials publicly doubted that enough alcohol could be produced to meet the continued increasing demand (the target of 1984 of 10.7×10^9 litres is still unchanged). At the same time the government has put the price of ethanol to the maximum level allowed by law: that is 68% of the price of gasoline. As a result sales of alcohol-fuelled vehicles have slumped and are not expected to have exceeded 140000 units in 1981. Moreover, it is estimated that the production of alcohol is falling behind schedule by almost 2 years. A 1981 target of 4.7×10^9 litres per year will be short by 0.5×10^9 litres and the 1982 supply is estimated at 4.5×10^9 litres and will be 1×10^9 litres less than planned. By 1985 the production may not reach 80% of the target of 10.7×10^9 litres per year.

Although some 390 distillery projects have already been approved bringing the Brazilian installed capacity to 9.1×10^9 litres, there is too much emphasis on this production from sugarcane—probably 95%. Additionally there is also too high a concentration of these projects in the State of São Paulo which is only 3% of Brazil's land area yet is to produce 65% of the alcohol.

The initial sales boom in the alcohol-fuelled cars seems to have rapidly subsided, the 140000 cars sold in 1981 is well below the 360000 maximum set by the government. Only a total of 440000 alcohol-fuelled cars exist in 1982 as against the expected government figure of 1 million. A combination of reasons may be responsible. In April/May 1980, ethanol fuel was only 35% of the gasoline price, moreover it was sold on Saturdays when gasoline stations were closed. Owners of alcohol-fuelled cars paid lower vehicle registration taxes and obtained better financing terms (36 months against 12 months) for car purchase. It was feared that the Iraq–Iran war threatened Brazil's oil-supply. These reasons for the initial boom sending buyers scrambling for alcohol-powered cars have largely disappeared and the current low oil prices and varying degrees of glut surplus have reversed the situation. Instead conflicting government priorities, varying economic policies, balance of payments problems, varying energy balances and fears of alcohol shortage have swung the situation over again. In addition too much petrol is being exported to the United States, and there appears to be a government policy of restricting personal vehicle utilization by the higher fuel prices, taxes and purchase taxes. Complaints by drivers of alcohol-fuelled cars have been played up by the Press: these range from poor performance, engine corrosion, costly maintenance to rapid deterioration, and have also fuelled the recessional situation.

Nevertheless, in spite of these problems, there is still room for optimism. The recession appears to be bottoming out, the car manufacturers are predicting a 10% increase in sales in 1983 and a 10% increase in the ethanol-chemical industry. New projects now on-stream are demanding another 0.5×10^9 litres and will ensure that at least this sector will consume 650 million litres by 1985. In addition, in September 1981 Brazil's largest ethanol-to-ethylene plant came on-stream in Alagoas with an installed capacity of 60000 tonnes per year of alcohol. It is the first industrial-scale ethylene plant and represents a clear turning point away from hydrocarbon feedstocks for the chemical industry. The purity of the ethylene is 100% and is totally from renewable biological starting materials. It will be used to produce ethylene chloride for vinyl-chloride monomer and to produce polyvinyl chloride.

The final comment can only be that the energy projects in Brazil are probably the most ambitious in the world— certainly the Third World—and in the present world climate are bound to go through a period of political and economic crisis and criticism.

APPENDIX 1   BRAZIL: BASIC DATA

A1.1   National Statistics and Demographic Data (see Tables A1.1 and A1.2)

A1.2   Non-Biomass Energy Sources in Brazil

A1.2.1   *Domestic Oil Production*

Estimates of reserves vary considerably since much exploration needs to be done. Vast investments are being made in research, prospecting and the drilling of new wells by *Petrobrás* (the State oil company) and other companies which have signed service contracts with risk clauses. Known domestic oil reserves total 1495 million barrels but oil in non-commercial quantities has been found off the Amazon Delta and in the Amazon jungles. It is estimated that daily average output will reach 260 thousand barrels in 1982. Natural gas reserves are put at 45.1×10^9 m^3.

A1.2.2   *Electricity*

Hydroelectric energy already accounts for 25% of Brazil's primary energy, and is a source which can be vastly improved. In terms of immediate and low cost utilization, the Brazilian estimated hydro-electric potential capacity now stands at 213000 MW of which only 28000 MW (some 13%) are now installed. A considerable proportion of this is concentrated in the giant Itaipu dam on the Paraná River and the other in the Tocantin's River—the Tucuruí dam—in the Amazonia. Electricity consumption rose from 71510 GWh in 1974 to 115040 GWh in 1980 (estimated) with an annual growth of 12.6%.

Hydrothermal capacity rose from 22279 MW in 1976 to 33834 MW in 1980 (estimated), with an annual growth rate 1976-1980 of 21.4%.

The Itaipu Hydroelectric Plant, a joint Brazilian-Paraguayan project, is scheduled to be put into operation in 1983/84, adding 12600 MW to the installed generating capacity. The Tucuruí Plant will only add in its first stage 3960 MW. It should be mentioned that electricity reserves are often between 2000-4000 km away from the main consuming centre, posing considerable transmission problems.

1	Territorial area (1000 km²)	8512
2	Population (millions)	122
	– Urban	81
	– Rural	41
3	Principal metropolitan areas (1000 inhabitants)	
	– Brasília (federal district)	1177
	– São Paulo	12719
	– Rio de Janeiro	9153
	– Belo Horizonte	2592
	– Recife	2401
	– Porto Alegre	2284
	– Salvador	1801
4	GDP: US$ 285.4 × 10⁹ (conversion at average exchange rate of year)[1]	
5	Per capita GDP: US$ 2339	
6	Net Domestic Product at factor costs (sectoral participation)	
	– Primary sector	12.1%
	– Secondary sector	31.9%
	– Tertiary sector	56.0%
7	Electrical Energy	
	– Installed capacity (MW)	37281
	– Consumption (GWh)	124393
8	University students enrolled (1000)	1470
9	Number of bank branches	14350
10	Trade Balance (US$ billions)	
	– Exports	23.3
	– Imports	21.1
11	Foreign Reserves (US$ billions)	7.5
12	Principal crops (1000 tons) (1980 figures)	
	– Cotton (in seed)	1673
	– Rice	97848
	– Cocoa (beans)	321
	– Coffee	1067
	– Sugarcane	146290
	– Maize (grain)	20374
	– Soybeans (grain)	15153
	– Wheat	2641
13	Industrial production	
	– Steel (1000 tons)	13200
	– Aircraft (units)	265
	– Automotive vehicles (units)	780800
	– Shipbuilding (1000 dwt)	1204
14	Exchange Rate Cr$/US$ at end of period)	

Year	Sale	Percentage change in relation to previous year
1974	7.435	19.53
1975	9.070	21.99
1976	12.345	36.11
1977	16.050	30.01
1978	20.920	30.34
1979	42.530	103.30
1980	65.500	54.01
1981	127.800	95.11

Source: 'Brazil: land of the present', European Bank Ltd., 1982.

[1] Preliminary data.

Table A1.2   Estimated population: 1980-2000 (million)

Age group	1980	1985	1990	1995	2000
0–4	19	22	24	26	29
5–9	17	20	22	25	28
10–14	14	17	20	23	26
15–19	13	14	17	20	23
20–24	12	13	14	17	20
25–29	9	11	13	14	17
30–34	8	10	11	13	14
35–39	6	8	10	11	13
40–44	5	6	8	10	11
45–49	5	5	6	8	9
50–54	4	5	5	6	7
55–59	3	4	4	5	6
60–64	2	3	4	4	5
65–69	2	2	3	3	4
70–74	1	1	2	2	3
75–79	0.7	1	1	1	2
80+	0.4	0.5	0.7	1	1
Total	121.1	142.5	164.7	189	218

Source: Based on *Fundação Instituto Brasileiro de Geografia e Estatística* figures.

Urban/rural population division: per cent

	1970	1975	1980
Urban	44	40	36
Rural	56	60	64
Total	100	100	100

Source: IBGE.

Estimated population by region by 1980 (millions)

North	4.9
North East	36.2
South East	51.6
South	22.5
Centre West	7.8
Total	123.0

Source: Coulson, 1980.

The Plan of Electrical Energy Needs, covering up to 1995—which is an integral part of Brazil's energy policy, foresees a total investment of Cr$1.5 × 10^{12} between 1980-1990, excluding financial charges and the expenditures on projects in construction, but scheduled to go on line after 1990. Taking into account the 33400 MW of the fifteen plants under construction, the installed capacity of Brazil's plants will be 77500 MW in 1990. Such investment will need to be financed to a great extent from abroad which will pose serious problems to the already large balance of payments problem now facing Brazil.

A1.2.3 *Nuclear Energy*

Brazilian industry tends to be concentrated in the south-east of the country, where the hydroelectric potential is nearing exhaustion. The energy required to maintain the region's economic growth will require the transmission of electricity, at great expense, from Amazonia, or, as the pro-nuclear lobby argues, the use of nuclear power.

Brazil has opted, in any case, for a programme of nuclear energy. The country would not depend on foreign sources of uranium (although it will be dependent on foreign technology) since current domestic reserves are estimated at 215000 tons of U_3O_8. Brazil's controversial nuclear-power programme is based on one 600 MW Westinghouse reactor and up to eight 1300 MW reactors from Kraftwork Union. However, by 1980 the programme was already 2 years behind schedule and a growing body of opinion publicly questions the value of expending the very large sums required, at a time when savings are being demanded everywhere else.

The first reactor—Angra I—sited on the coast between Rio and São Paulo was not expected to start producing, at the earliest, before early 1981. Construction has started on the Angra II on the same site, the first of the German reactors set for 1987 and the third plant will follow in a further 8 months. Taken together these units will produce a total of 3200 MW. When the fourth and fifth units—location studies are now in progress—go into operation, another 2400 MW will be added to the total.

To complete the fuel cycle, Brazil has already placed contracts for the uranium enrichment and processing plants. In 1987 the enrichment plant is expected to possess an industrial production capacity and become commercially operable in 1991.

It is expected that the next decade will be one of the most financially difficult that Brazil has faced and thus, in spite of the estimated $8 × 10^9 that will have been spent by then, nuclear power will be contributing no more than 2.5% of all energy being produced in Brazil.

A1.2.4 *Coal and Shale*

Coal reserves are put at 22×10^9 tons, although other estimates put it as high as 80×10^9 tons. Unfortunately its coal contains very high ash content (sulphur) and is generally of poorer quality than typical British coals.

Of bituminous shale, Brazil possesses the world's second largest reserves totalling 532.4×10^9 m^3 located at almost ground level extening through practically the whole southern region of the country, although reserves have also been located in the central-west, north and north-east.

Petrobras is already preparing an industrial plant for the production of oil from coal in São Mateus do Sul (State of Paraná). The first and second stages of the construction should be completed in 1983 and 1985 respectively. When the unit comes into full operation, it will have a daily production capacity of 51000 barrels of crude oil, plus 500 tons of liquid gas and 900 tons of other chemicals.

A1.3 Foreign Investment in Brazil

The participation by foreign capital in any sector of Brazil's economy is always controversial. It provokes fears that market conditions may be radically changed as a result, forcing national enterprises out of business, or placing them under foreign control. However, historically speaking, foreign investment has been a major fact of life in the manufacturing sector of Brazil.

Table A1.3 conveniently summarizes foreign investment in Brazil up to the end of 1981. A sectoral investment analysis demonstrates that the major share of foreign capital has been marshalled into the different segments of the manufacturing industry (74.0%) of the 19.247×10^9 of total investment. In 1981, alone, this area of industrial activity received 14×10^9 in investment.

The high rate of participation of foreign investment in the areas of basic chemical products (14%), transport equipment (13.5%), mechanics (9.5%), electrical and communications equipment (7.7%), and metallurgy (7.1%) seems to have been due to the programmes undertaken to substitute imports of capital goods and basic imports, as well as the expansion of the automotive industry. Of the total registered investments and reinvestments, 20.1% was channelled into the service sector of the economy. This results from the fact that 1.6×10^9 was allocated to such segments as consulting services, representation, participation, property administration and advertising (in 1979).

Despite its declining participation in recent years, the US continues to hold the major share (30.2%) of foreign investment; West Germany

Table A.1.3   Foreign investments in Brazil. Distribution according
to areas of activity. (Position on 31 December 1981.)
US$ Millions

Area of activity	Investments	Reinvestments	Total	Total (%)
Mineral extraction industry	458	69	527	2.7
Manufacturing industry	9460	4794	14254	74
Chemicals	1833	872	2705	14
Transport equipment	1695	899	2594	13.5
Mechanics	1415	405	1820	9.5
Electrical and communications equipment	957	525	1482	7.7
Metallurgy	988	394	1382	7.1
Other	2572	1699	4271	22.2
Services	3169	705	3874	20.1
Other	446	146	592	3.0
Total	13533	5714	19247	100

Source: 'Brazil: land of the present', European Brazilian Bank Ltd., 1982.

follows (with 13.5%), Switzerland (10.4%) and Japan (9.4%) (which has
increased its presence in the last few years). These same countries
were responsible for about 60% of the capital stock added to the
balance existing at the end of 1978.

A1.4 Useful Addresses related to the Alcohol Industry

(1) Comissão Executiva Nacional do Álcool (CENAL)
     Ministério da Indústria e do Comércio
     Esplanada dos Ministérios
     Bloco B–Sala 920
     Brazilia–DF–CEP: 70053

(2) Instituto do Açúcar e do Álcool (IAA)
     Ministério da Indústria e do Comércio
     Sede: Praqa XV de Novembro
     42-7° Andar
     Rio de Janeiro–RJ–CEP: 20010

     Regional Offices (IAA)

     São Paulo
     Rua Formosa
     367-21° Andar
     São Paulo–SP–CEP: 01049

Pernambuco
AV. Dantas Barreto
324-8° Andar
Recife-PE-CEP: 50000

Alagoas
Rua do Comércio
115/121-8° Andar
Maceió-AL-CEP: 57000

Minas Gerais
AV. Afonso Pena
867-9° Andar
Belo Horizonte-MG-CEP: 30000

(3) Secretaria de Tecnología Industrial (STI)
Ministério da Indústria e do Comércio
Setor de Autarquias Sul
Quadra 2
Bloco 2
Brasilia-DF-CEP: 70053

(4) Empresa Brasileira de Assistencia
Técnica e Extensão Rural (Embrater)
Ministério da Agricultura
Sector de Edificios Públicos Norte
AV W/3 Norte, Quadra 515, Lote 3
Brasilia-DF-CEP: 70770

(5) Banco Nacional do Desenvolvimento
Económico (BNDE)
AV. Rio Branco 53
Rio de Janeiro-RJ-CEP: 20090

Regional Branches
Conj: 251 A/C
50-25° Andar
AV. São Luiz
São Paulo-SP-CEP: 01046

North East
Rua Riachuelo
105-7° Andar
Recife-PE-CEP: 50000

Federal District
Sector Bancário Sul-conj: 1-Bloco E
13° Andar
Brasília-DF-CEP: 70000

(6) Banco do Brasil SA
Departmento de Normas e Asúntos
Industriais (DENAI)
Divisão de Análise de Projectos Industriais
Edificio Sede — 7° Andar
Sector Bancário Sul
Brasília-DF–CEP: 70073

Regional Branches (ALL)
São Paulo
Av. Paulista
2163-12° Andar
São Paulo-SP-CEP: 01311

(7) Banco Nacional de Crédito Cooperativo (BNCC)
SBN Edificio Palácio do Besenvolvimento
2° Andar
Brasília-DF–CEP: 70057

(8) *State Development Banks* (All states have them)

Ceará
Banco de Desenvolvimento do Ceará SA (BANDECE)
Rua Senador Pompeu
834-4° Andar
Fortaleza-CE–CEP: 60000

São Paulo
Banco de Desenvolvimento do Estado de São Paulo
SA (BADESP)
Av. Paulista
1776-1°/6° Andares
São Paulo-SP-CEP: 01310

Minas Gerais
Banco de Desenvolvimento de Minas Gerais (BDMG)
Rua da Bahia, 1600
Belo Horizonte-MG–CEP: 20000

Rio de Janeiro
Banco de Desenvolvimento do Estado do Rio de Janeiro
(BD-RIO)
Praia do Flamengo, 200
23°/25° Andares
Rio de Janeiro-RJ–CEP: 22210

Bahia
Banco de Desenvolvimento do Estado da Bahia
SA (DESENBANCO)
AV. Magalhães Neto, S/Nº
Salvador-BA-CEP: 40000

British firms supplying technology etc. to Brazil's agrochemical sector

(9) Humphreys & Glasgow Limited
22 Carlisle Place
London
SW1P 1JA
Tel: 01-828 1234   Telex: 261821

(Has a number of contacts in Brazil dealing with the agro-chemicals.)

(10) Imperial Chemical Industries (ICI)
Imperial Chemical House
Millbank
London
Tel: (01) 834 4444   Telex: 21324

(Trades with Brazil across the whole spectrum of products)
Their representative in Brazil is:

Cia Imperial de Industrias Quimicas do Brasil
(ICI-BRAZIL)
AV. Euzebio Matoso
891-2 Andar
Edificio das Naçoes
05423 São Paulo-SP

(11) *Tate & Lyle Group* seems to be the British Company most involved in supplying equipment and technology to the Brazilian alcohol and sugar industries.

(a) *Sugar Factory Machinery*
A & W Smith & Co Limited
Eglimton Works
Cook Street
Glasgow
G5 8GW
Tel: 041 429 5441   Telex: 77137

Smith equipment manufactured under licence—including complete Alcohol Distilleries—in Brazil by:

(b) Companhia Siderurgica Do Nordeste (COSINOR)
Rua Da Aurora 1481/1503
Caixa Postal 163
50000 Recife
Pernambuco
Brazil
Tel: 231 4145   Telex: 1215

(c) New Process Technology, Control Equipment and Speciality Chemicals:

Tate & Lyle Process Technology
55 Liddon Road
Bromley
BR1 2SR
Tel: 01 460 9900   Telex: 896253

(d) Consultancy and Technical Services:

Tate & Lyle Technical Services Limited
Enterprise House
45 Homesdale Road
Bromley Common
Bromley
BR2 9TE
Tel: 01 464 6556   Telex: 896368

Talycopi
Rua da Aurora 1481/1503
Caixa Postal 163
50000 Recife
Pernambuco
Brazil
Tel: 231 4145   Telex: (081) 1215

(e) *Technical Services and Speciality Products of Brazilian Manufacture:*

Tate & Lyle do Brasil Ltd.
Praca Olavo Bilac
28-S 510
20000 Rio de Janeiro-RJ
Brazil
Tel: 224 0545   Telex: 2122102

(12) *Brazilian engineering and consultancy companies in the alcohol field. Quimica e Derivados* recently listed the following as significant.

BRASÁLCOOL
Empresa Brasileira de Álcool S/A
rua Hungria, 888
9° Andar
Tel: 210-6111/211-6488, São Paulo, SP.

COMPANHIA DE TECNOLOGIA INDUSTRIAL
av. Venezuela, 82
Tel: 253-9294, Rio de Janeiro, R.J.

CONTERMA
Construtora Industrial e Termotécnica S/A
rua Capote Valente, 1336
Tel: 864-1155, São Paulo, SP.

COPERSUCAR
Cooperative Central dos Produtores de Açúcar e Álcool do
Estado de São Paulo
rua Boa Vista, 280
4° Andar
Tel: 229-0611, São Paulo, SP.

EQUIPLAN
Consultoria e Planejamento S/C Ltda.
av. Rebouças, 2 066
Tel: 881-8111, São Paulo, SP.

FAZANARO SA
Industrial e Comercial
rua Bom Jesus, 1 663
Tel: 33-9255/33-2455, Piracicaba, SP.

METALÚRGICA BARBOSA LTDA.
rua Zeferino Bacchi, 288
Tel: 33-2991/33-1901, Piracicaba, SP.

MONTREAL
Engenharia S/A
rua São José, 90
7° Andar
Tel: 291-6116, Rio de Janeiro, RJ.

NATRON
Consultoria e Projetos S/A
rue Teófilo Ottoni, 61/63
11° Andar
Tel: 233-0322/233-5552, Rio de Janeiro, RJ.

PLANAL
Consultoria & Projeto
rue XV de Novembro, 944
6° Andar
Tel: 22-5959/33-8087, Piracicaba, SP.

PROMON
Engenharia S/A
av. Nove de Julho, 4 939
Tel: 282-7944/280-8044, São Paulo, SP.

PROQUIP
Projetos e Engenharia Industrial S/A
av. Rebouças, 2 258
Tel: 280-3177, São Paulo, SP.

SACAROTÉCNICA
Consultoria, Estudos e Projetos Ltda.
rua Cons. Crispiniano, 344
7° Andar
Tel: 222-5311, São Paulo, SP.

SONDOTÉCNICA
Engenharia de Solos Ltda.
largos dos Leões, 15
Tel: 246-4173/286-8544, Rio de Janeiro, RJ.

SUCRAL
Assessoria e Projetos para Açúcar e Álcool S/C Ltda.
praça José Bonifácio, 799
3° Andar
Tel: 22-3061/22-3062, Piracicaba, SP.

APPENDIX 2

Table A2.1(a) Ethyl alcohol condensed data

	Units		Ref.
Physical properties			
Molecular weight		46.07	
Melting point	°C	−114.4	1
	°F	−173.9	
Boiling point	°C	78.4	2
	°F	173.1	
Specific gravity at 60°/60°F		0.794	2
Viscosity at 20°C	centipoises	1.22	1
Refractive index at 20°C		1.3614	3
Surface tension at 20°C	dynes/cm	22.5	1
Explosive limits in air			4
Lower	vol %	3.9	
Upper	vol %	19.0	
Flash-point—open cup,			
approximate	°F	70	2
Auto ignition temperature	°F	738	4
Solubility			
In water		complete	
Water in		complete	
Colour		colourless	
Coefficient of expansion			2
Per °C		0.00113	
Per °F		0.00063	
Thermodynamic properties			
Thermal conductivity	BTU/(hr) (sq ft) (°F/ft)	0.105	5
Specific heat at 68°F	BTU/lb/°F	0.573	6
Heat of combustion at 20°C	Kcal/mole	327.6	7
	BTU/lb	12800	
Heat of formation at 25°C	Kcal/mole	−66.356	8
Free energy of formation			
at 25°C	Kcal/mole	−41.77	8
Entropy at 25°C	cal/mole °K	38.4	8
Heat of fusion at MP	Kcal/mole	1.187	9
	BTU/lb	46.37	
Heat of vaporization at BP	Kcal/mole	9.410	9
Critical temperature	°C	243.1	9
	°F	469.6	

Table A2.1 (*cont.*)

	Units			*Ref.*
Critical pressure	atm	63.1		9
	psia	927.3		
Critical density	gm/ml		0.2755	9
	lb/cu ft		17.19	

Source: Basic Physical Properties of Ethyl Alcohol. Ref. *Ethyl Alcohol Handbook*, USI Chemicals, 1969.

References

1 A. K. Doolittle (1954), *The Technology of Solvents and Plasticizers*, New York: John Wiley & Sons, Inc.
2 U.S. Industrial Chemicals Co.
3 N. A. Lange (1956), *Handbook of Chemistry*, Sandusky: Handbook Publishers, Inc.
4 J. H. Perry (1950), *Chemical Engineers' Handbook*, New York: McGraw-Hill Co., Inc.
5 O. C. Bates *et al.* (1938), 'Thermal Conductivity of Liquids', *Analytical Chemistry*, 10, 314–18.
6 J. Timmermans (1950), *Physico-Chemical Constants of Pure Organic Compounds*, New York: Elsevier.
7 N. A. Lange (1956), *Handbook of Chemistry*, Sandusky: Handbook Publishers, Inc.
8 U.S. Department of Commerce (1952), *Selected Values of Chemical Thermodynamic Properties, N.B.S. Circular 500*, Washington: Govt. Printing Office.
9 J. H. Perry (1950), *Chemical Engineers' Handbook*, New York: McGraw-Hill Book Co., Inc.

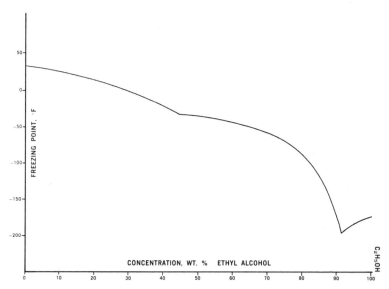

Fig. A2.1   Freezing point of ethyl alcohol—water mixtures. *Source*: A. Seidell, *Solubilities of Organic Compounds* (New York: D. Van Nostrand Co., Inc., 1941), 2, 129-30.

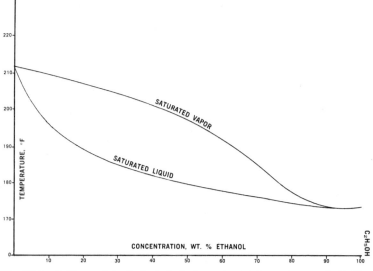

Fig. A2.2   Boiling point of ethyl alcohol—water mixtures. *Source*: J. C. Chu *et al., Vapor-Liquid Equilibrium Data* (Ann Arbor: J. W. Edwards, 1956).

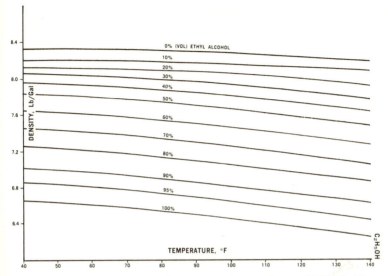

Fig. A2.3 Density of ethyl alcohol—water mixtures. *Source*: E. W. Washburn *et al., International Critical Tables of Numerical Data, Physics, Chemistry and Technology* (New York: McGraw Hill, 1933).

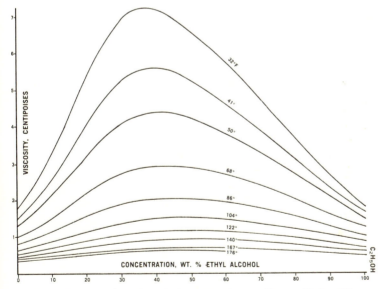

Fig. A2.4 Viscosity of ethyl alcohol—water mixtures. *Source: National Bureau of Standards Bulletin, 14* (1918), 59.

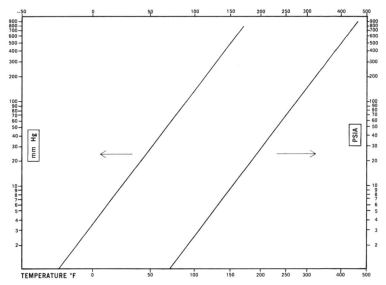

Fig. A2.5 Vapour pressure of ethyl alcohol. *Source*: D. R. Stull, 'Vapor Pressure of Pure Substances—Organic Compounds', *Industrial and Engineering Chemistry*, 39 (1947), 517–40.

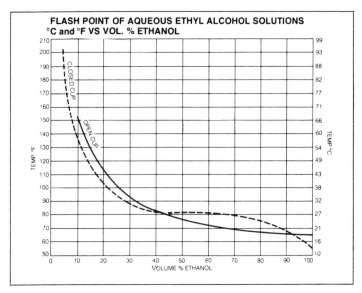

Fig. A2.6 Flash point of aqueous ethyl alcohol. *Source*: U.S. Industrial Chemicals Co., Tuscola, Illinois.

APPENDIX 3   ORDERS OF MAGNITUDE AND CONVERSION FACTORS

Orders of magnitude
   kilo = 10^3; mega = 10^6; giga = 10^9; tera = 10^{12}; peta = 10^{15};
   exa = 10^{18}; micro (μ) = 10^{-6}; nano (n) = 10^{-9}

Energy
   1 MJ = 0.27778 kWh = 238.85 kcal = 947.92 BTU = 0.37251 hph.
   1 tce (ton coal equivalent) = 27.9 GJ
   1 tpe (tonne petroleum equivalent) = 7.5 barrels (North Sea Crude)
   = 44.8 GJ
   1000 ft^3 natural gas = 28.3 m^3 natural gas = 1.1 GJ

Area
   1 hectare = 2.47 acres = 10^4 m^2

Volume
   1 m^3 = 1000 litres = 35.315 ft^3 = 219.97 UK gallons = 264.17
   US gallons

Mass
   1 kg = 2.205 lbs = 0.001 tonne (t)
   1 tonne = 0.984 tons = 1.102 short tons = 1000 kg = 2205 lbs

Power
   1 W = 1 Js^{-1} = 0.001 kW = 0.001341 hp

AUTHOR INDEX

SUBJECT INDEX